# The Lessons of Love

D0096433

### Don't Quit

When things go wrong as they sometimes will,
When the road you're trudging seems all uphill,
When the funds are low, and the debts are high,
And you want to smile, but you have to sigh,
When care is pressing you down a bit—
Rest if you must, but don't you quit.

Success is failure turned inside out,
The silver tint of the clouds of doubt,
And you never can tell how close you are,
It may be near when it seems afar.
So, stick to the fight when you're hardest hit—
It's when things go wrong that you mustn't quit.

Author Unknown

THIS BOOK BELONGS TO

*Evelyn L. Dodge*

Also available in Large Print from
Walker and Company

*Codependent No More*

# The Lessons of Love

## REDISCOVERING OUR PASSION FOR LIFE
## WHEN IT ALL SEEMS TOO HARD TO TAKE

Melody Beattie

Walker and Company
New York

Large Print edition published by arrangement with Harper San Francisco, a Division of Harper Collins Publishers, 1995.

Published simultaneously in Canada by Thomas Allen & Son Canada, Limited, Markham, Ontario.

Library of Congress Cataloging-in-Publication Data
Beattie, Melody.
The lessons of love : rediscovering our passion for life when it all seems too hard to take / Melody Beattie. — 1st large print ed.
    p.    cm.
  ISBN 0-8027-2685-2 (lg. print)
  1. Consolation.  2. Bereavement—Religious aspects.  I. Title.
[BV4905.2.B337    1995]
158'. 1—dc20                        94-44339
                                             CIP

Grateful acknowledgment is made to Leiber and Stoller and to Warner/Chappell Music, Inc., for permission to quote lyrics from "Stand By Me" by Ben E. King, Mike Stoller, and Jerry Leiber, copyright © 1961 Jerry Leiber Music, Mike Stoller Music & Unichappell Music (Renewed). All rights reserved. Used by permission.

First Large Print Edition, 1995
Walker and Company
435 Hudson Street
New York, New York  10014

Printed in the United States of America

10   9   8   7   6   5   4   3   2   1

This book is dedicated to
Nichole Marie Beattie
and
Shane Anthony Beattie

# Contents

....................

# Acknowledgments

· · · · · · · · · · · · · · · · · · ·

For their help in making this book possible, I want to acknowledge and thank:

Christie, the children's nanny and our housekeeper. She loved and cared for the children when I couldn't be there to do that.

John Hanson, Shane's best friend, and his mother Sue.

David, the children's father.

My mother, who again told me, "You can do it."

My family—Jeanne, Joanne, and Jimmy—and their spouses, who opened their hearts to me and with whom I became delightfully reacquainted.

John Thurik.

Nan, a gentle light during a dark time.

Wendylee, for her strength, encouragement, and support.

Ann Poe, for coming back into my life as an editor and a friend.

Caroline Pincus, Tom Grady, Clayton Carlson, and the rest of the Harper staff, for their vision for this book and their belief in me.

Erin, a gentle reminder about the gifts of an open heart.

Max.

Echo, my best girlfriend, for her love, support, and many healing gifts.

Echo's brother and my friend, Mike.

Megan, with her freckled face and cherub smile.

The Cooks.

God.

The many healing professionals who kept me alive while I decided to come back to life: Dr. Bill, Dr. Steve, Dr. Gary, Peg, Chris, and the staff at Life Force.

Jeanie Reinert, for yellow roses, Charlie, and the story that helped me believe in mine.

Ahmos, my manager, who continually believed in me and my future, even when I didn't.

Louie, my best man friend, who came to help open my heart and teach me about love.

The Get Along Gang: Joey, Carmen, Ingrid, and Ray.

David Hackler, an inspiration and a survivor.

Nichole, for her love, presence, and dedication. I couldn't have done this without you, baby.

Shane, for the many gifts that still live on.

And Scotty, my warrior and knight. You

cation. I couldn't have done this without you, baby.

Shane, for the many gifts that still live on.

And Scotty, my warrior and knight. You came along just when I needed you most.

But then you all did, didn't you?

# Introduction

· · · · · · · · · · · · · · · · · · · ·

"It's not the passage of time that heals,"
he whispered. "It's the passage through
experiences."

IT'S A FRIDAY EVENING IN FEBRUARY 1991. I'M at a comedy gallery in downtown St. Paul with my daughter Nichole and a few friends. My friend Louie Anderson is doing a special performance. I listen some. Even laugh a bit. Louie always makes me laugh. Then he closes the show with a simple line, "Shane, we love you," and walks offstage.

Louie, who's been with us all week, heads back to California. Nichole and I begin the forty-five-minute drive from St. Paul to Stillwater, the small town where we've lived for seven years. It's an unorthodox ending to a strange day. My son Shane has been fatally injured in a ski accident. This is the evening of his funeral.

I go home, lie down, and wonder where people go when they die. I am about to learn. Two years later, I realize that it isn't my son Shane who needs raising from the dead, as Jesus raised Lazarus. By then I will conclude that Shane is safe on the other side.

It's me that needs resurrection.

Change is constant. But the change

wrought by some moments is more profound than others. Sometimes we turn a corner. Sometimes we're pushed off a cliff. We aren't facing our worst fears; we're living through them.

This seeming fall from grace may be triggered by one traumatic incident. Or it may be a slow grinding away of passion and hope until all that's left isn't bittersweet—it's plain bitter. Life has repeatedly disappointed us, and we can't seem to pull out of it. It's not that our faith is weakened; it's that we don't believe in life anymore.

The magic is gone.

I'm a journalist, an author, a mother, a woman. *The Lessons of Love* is my sixth book. It's the most difficult book I've written, the first in the intervening years since Shane's death. It's a story about what I've learned and seen about life and love since I got pushed off that cliff.

Recently, when I was getting my nails done, the manicurist asked me what I was working on. When I started to tell her, she scrunched her face. "Not a gloom-and-doom book," she said.

"No," I said, "it isn't."

This is a love story. Not about the fluffy kind of love. About the raw kind. The kind that makes us grow, change, expand, and move on. It's a real-life love story.

Writing it has become a profound experience, more so than I anticipated when I took on the project. It's not the mere tapping out of words, for I've scribbled hundreds of thousands of words in my life. The problem isn't the exercise of technical skills. And, although I usually learn something about myself and life when I write, I'm not writing this book as therapy, a chance to purge my emotions. I do that other ways.

The challenge I face is that writing this book forces me to embrace the ideas I'm writing about. To write this book I must come fully alive, care about life, heal my own soul, for creativity is life-giving and demands that of us. To write this book, I must make the same shift in my writing that I've made in my life, that of moving from my head to my heart.

As many of us know, that shift can be intense.

*The Lessons of Love* is about rekindling the flames of passion when the embers begin to cool. It's about letting ourselves see, touch, feel, and taste life's magic again when we think all the magic is gone and probably never existed in the first place. It's about swallowing pride and fear and having the guts and the tenacity to have faith when we've been stripped of naïveté and shaken to the core—when we know too well that life isn't just mysterious and unpredictable, it can be unbearably cruel and breathtakingly wondrous, sometimes at the same time.

*The Lessons of Love* isn't a grief book, although that's part of it, for grieving is inherently and mysteriously connected to loving deeply. It's a book about opening the heart, living from the heart, trusting the heart. It's a learning-to-live-again book. It's a story about love's ultimate and absolute lesson: that love is the only thing in this world that cannot be lost because it's the only thing that's real.

And sometimes love hurts.

It's for anyone who wonders if love, or life, is worthwhile.

It's for anyone who's been forced to start over one more time.

It's for anyone who's been pushed off the cliff.

. . . . . . .

Clarissa Pinkola Estès, in her beautiful little book *The Gift of Story,* describes stories, particularly those that rise from suffering, as powerful healing medicines, remedies that can teach, lighten, assist transformation, heal wounds, and recreate memory.

Homeopathic medicines, natural remedies for disease that produce symptoms similar to the disease they're being used to cure, are regaining popularity. Many of us know instinctively that stories are homeopaths for the soul.

That's why I'm writing this book in story form.

In a world that can foster cynicism and disillusionment, some of us still want to believe. In a world that uses words like *relationships* and *parenting skills,* some of us still prefer the other one, the more ancient one: *love.*

One cold night, in the late hours, because

that's when we usually talk, my friend Scotty told me this story. I was raging and whimpering, trying to convince him that life was too hard, that I couldn't do it, couldn't start over again one more time. What he said, the story he told me, is the story I now tell you:

In a mysterious land, not so far away, and in a time not that long ago, word spread of a man called the Alchemist. In his presence, things transformed. He could, some said, turn a single dry bone of a deer into a green forest, alive with rushing water, wind, sunshine, grass, and a gentle doe nuzzling her fawn. He could turn pain, tragedy, agony—spiritual voids and angst of the worst kind—into laughter, healing, a joy so gentle yet deep that it rocked the soul. And hope, the purest, sweetest gift of all.

He could turn the basest metal into gold.

One day, having heard of this magic, an angry young man pounded on the

Alchemist's door, demanding that his ore be turned into gold.

"Why?" asked the Alchemist.

"I need money to pay bills. Now hurry!" the young man huffed.

The Alchemist turned him away.

A second time the young man returned, again demanding gold.

Asked why, he sputtered, "Why must you even ask?"

Again his request was denied.

On his third visit, the young man knocked more gently.

"Please don't turn me away," he said. "I need gold to buy a ring, a gift for my beloved."

This time, his wish was granted.

This book is my gold ring for you.

# Part I

# One

"You don't blast a heart open," she said. "You coax and nurture it open, like the sun does to a rose."

A CANDLE BURNS BY MY COMPUTER. PACHEL-bel's "Canon in D" plays on the radio. A light snowfall covers the ground.

It's almost Christmas.

I'm writing in my bedroom at a small desk. I closed the curtains because the glare makes it hard to see. And because it feels warmer that way.

Max, my bird, sits on a laundry basket in front of a mirror. She likes the mirror. She likes being near me.

The phone rings. It's Scotty.

"How are you coming with the book?" he asks.

The question runs deep. How are you doing with your life? is what he's really asking. How are you doing with faith, hope, confidence. Caring about life. Getting back up. Trying again. The simple, beautiful act of trying.

"Not good," I say. "I'm stuck."

What I mean is, I feel forgotten by God, like Sisyphus, condemned to pushing a rock up a hill, only to have it roll down before it reaches the top. I feel alienated, abandoned, afraid of being tricked or betrayed.

What I also don't say is that I've been begging God, the universe, the Force, Allah, Etah, to show me what it is I'm not seeing, what I'm doing wrong.

I've lost my voice, my writing voice. I can't hear my heart.

"I'm flying in," he says. "I'm coming back."

I argue with him for a while. No, you can't come, I have to work. No, all we do is play. No, you're a distraction. We hang up. I used to feel guilty when I said no. Now it's all I can say. No. No. No.

I stare at the computer. I want to see him. Almost ashamed, I realize I need to see him. How can I trust what I want?

I pick up the phone. "Please come," I say.

At 9:30 that evening I meet him at the gate at the Minneapolis airport. We kiss. Banter. Kiss.

The next day I surprise myself when he asks what I want to do.

I look at him and say softly, "I want my ring back. I want to wear my ring again." The awakening has come gently.

I remember a time, nine years past. Another lifetime, it seems. I was married to someone else then and writing a book about owning your power, taking care of yourself, loving yourself. I went to my office, a basement cubbyhole in a small tract house, and began to write. As the words poured out, I arose from my cubbyhole, walked into the kitchen, looked at my husband of ten years, and quietly announced, "It's time for us to separate. To get divorced."

He agreed. The marriage had been dead for years. That it was time to bury it didn't surprise either one of us. We knew it was coming. I was learning that the part in me that writes, the part I must go to if I am to do anything but blather on paper, must be acknowledged and honored in my life before it can be expressed to the world.

Writing forces consciousness.

Those lessons nine years ago had been different in some ways. I wasn't allowed, I didn't allow myself, to write a book about independence, freedom, and self-worth unless I lived that way.

Now, I won't let myself write a book about

love, about being a vital part of a living universe, unless I live that way. The new way. Vitally. Magically.

One lesson is the same: listening to and trusting my voice.

A phrase haunts me; I can't recall where I heard it. **Love will never keep us from our destiny. It will lead us into it.**

I remember a telephone conversation several months ago with Scotty. "Do you feel you're being disloyal to your past by loving me?" he asked.

I didn't answer. I started crying.

"You don't need to say anything," he said. "And we don't need to discuss it. But I wanted to mention it, get it out in the open."

I wonder how long I've fought this lesson, fought opening up. Maybe the entire three months I've sat shriveled in front of the computer, glaring at the blank screen and the blinking cursor. Then I remember another truth. We have as much time as we need.

What happened to the woman I used to be, the woman who didn't need anyone? Maybe it's time to bury her now, too.

Scotty and I go to the store where we

bought our first rings a year and a half ago, simple gold bands scrolled with the words *Vous et Nul Autre.* You and no other. Shakespearian poesy rings.

Gold rings, a theme in my life.

I get scared. Twice we leave the store without the rings and wander around the mall. Can I commit to anything? A book? A person? Can I commit to life? Do I want to risk caring about life again? Do I believe in loss or am I willing to trust . . . life?

That evening we watch Joseph Campbell on television. He talks about God, about loving God. He says when we open to loving a person, whether that person is a spouse, friend, or child, we open our hearts to loving God. He says when we let someone love us, we're opening our hearts to God's love. He says the acts are the same.

I decide that loving isn't for the faint. It's for the courageous.

"I want to wear the ring," I say quietly. "But I'm not sure what it means or where we're going."

"I'm not either," he says. "But I know one thing. Everything will work out fine."

We both laugh. We're learning a new meaning for everything will work out fine.

Scotty takes the ring out of the rose-colored velvet box. He kisses the ring, then touches it to his heart.

Scotty, almost my childhood sweetheart. Scotty, who took me to an old saloon in Colorado to show me a painting on a floor, the painting of a woman's face, drawn by a man who loved her so much he wanted to memorialize her for all eternity. Scotty, who showed me that men have hearts, that they love and dare to be romantic.

"I want you to remember one thing," he says, sliding the ring on my finger.

I smile and finish his sentence. "That you absolutely and completely love me," I say.

He breathes. Smiles. And says, "Yes."

We kiss.

It's a simple celebration of love, a quiet act of trust in the future. I know well there are no guarantees. I know this is a moment in time. I smile, remembering what a friend said, a newspaper reporter for a local paper, when I asked her about her marriage. She had been madly in love with her husband when she'd met him. They had gone through some trials before settling into another kind of love. Now four years had passed since their wedding.

"Oh, we've had our troubles," she said. "But I guess that in forty years, we'll still be lying next to each other in bed at night squabbling, fussing, and passionately loving each other."

The next day the words start to come— phrases, sentences, chapters. I look at Scotty.

"Thank you," I say.

"For what?" he asks.

"Just thank you."

I'm ready to write. The universe is dancing with me, playing with me again. I'm dancing with it. My heart is open. I can hear it. I can hear me. The magic is back.

Scotty leaves on a plane headed for California. The next morning, I open the bedroom drapes, letting in the light, the day. Life.

I stand at the window watching the sunrise. In the aftermath of our time together, the truth surfaces to consciousness, slowly but as brightly as the orange morning sun.

It isn't the words "I do" that give magic or meaning to life.

The magic is in the words "I am."

# Two

"To know the mind of God," she said, "listen to your heart."

I GO DOWNSTAIRS, FIX A CUP OF TEA, AND SIT at the marble library table. We use it as a dining room table now. It's a remnant from the past, one of the few that still fits.

I look around. My life is simple now, different from a year ago. New pictures are on the wall, prints of the masters: Monet, Chagall, van Gogh, Matisse. The books on the shelves are different: mysteries by Chandler and Queen, Arthurian legends, quantum physics for the layperson, books on grief and life after death.

Joey and Nichole sit chattering. They've been best friends since seventh grade, part of a group of best friends.

"Guess what my dad did?" Joey says. "He strung lights on the outside of the house this year. For the first time!"

Nichole and I look at each other.

"Tell him to take them down," Nichole says.

"Why?" Joey asks.

"It's an omen," Nichole says.

No! I want to scream. It wasn't the lights. It was the snow globe. That was the omen.

. . . . . . .

It was Christmas 1990. The best Christmas of our lives. Nichole was fourteen that year. Shane was eleven.

We were good together, the three of us. All our years together had been good, even the ones with welfare cheese, powdered milk, and midnight runs to the all-night grocery store so the neighbors wouldn't see us using food stamps. We'd usually get caught anyway. No matter which register I'd stand at, the line would form behind me and watch as the cashier waved the stamps in the air, complaining that they stuck together.

It didn't matter. It was worth it. We had each other.

This year was a year of celebration. We'd finally made it to the top of the mountain, the upward slope we'd been climbing of overcoming poverty and a broken family. Gradually my writing career had begun to pay off. I had gone from hawking my stories to the local daily for twenty-five dollars to the *New York Times* best-seller list. People called me an overnight success, but that wasn't true.

I'd been plugging away at my writing since 1979, experiencing all the failures and frustrations that come with developing any career.

This year I had finished two books, back to back, by June. Then I stopped working. Said I couldn't do any publicity. The demands were intense, the lifestyle lonely. I was tired. I missed the children and they missed me. We were at a pinnacle. There were slaps on the back and high fives for all, but it was time to be together.

So the three of us traveled across the state and the continent that year. We went to movies. Watched television. Went fishing.

By the time the Christmas holidays came, I was determined to get into the spirit of things. The season held a bittersweet tone. I knew it was time to get back to work soon. And as I watched the years roll by and the children grow up, I saw my dream of a traditional family slip away.

I was lonely, the way a woman gets when she's raising a family alone. Scared. Maybe desperate.

A haunting feeling had chased me all year.

It hit hard on my forty-second birthday. I knew I wasn't going to be here forever. If most people live to be eighty, I figured I had started the second half of my life. But where had the first half gone? Doesn't time fly when you're having fun and working hard. And learning life's lessons.

I began taking vitamins. Stopped drinking coffee. Got more health conscious.

Recently Nichole pranced into the kitchen while I was making coffee, which I'm drinking again. "I finally figured out what's wrong with you," she announced. "You're in a midlife crisis. That's why you've been doing all these weird things. You'll settle down in a few years," she assured me. "We learned about it in health class."

What was wrong ran deeper than that. I was beginning to face, or maybe run from, the inevitability of death.

It hit me hard one night. Shane and I were at the movie theater. We went to movies a lot. I was sitting there watching the show, acutely aware of his little-boy energy next to me. He was resting his feet on the back of the seat in front of him. I thought about scolding him then decided not to bother. No one was sitting there. Some things weren't worth fussing over.

I tried to focus my attention on watching the movie, but a thought ran through me like a shock: this isn't going to last forever. Time is racing by. My children have been such a big part of my life for so long, but someday they'll be gone, moving on with their lives. I'll be gone. And this night, sitting here at this movie, will be a memory.

**Make every moment count.**

Maybe that's why I was so determined to make this Christmas our best one ever.

We strung lights on the outside of the house. For years Shane had wanted to do it. For years I had said no. It seemed too complicated. This year I had enough money, so I took the time. We also bought a manger scene and set it up in the front yard, something else Shane had wanted to do. We drove around the Twin Cities, finding the right pieces: the right Mary, Joseph, wise men, and baby Jesus. We found some angels, a stall, and some hay to spread on the ground.

All our Christmases together had been

good, because we loved each other. Even the ones when we were the names on the tree at Kmart, the names people donate presents to. But this year was better. We gave back. We had repaid the welfare department for their help. We took our names off the Kmart tree and bought presents for other people.

Echo and I played Santa that year. She'd been my best girlfriend for nearly twenty years. She had been with me in the delivery room, holding my hand and coaching me when both children were born. This year we decided we needed to make an effort to get into the holiday spirit. We got up early in the morning and met at our favorite restaurant for pancakes. We made lists, trying to think of the perfect gift for each person.

A music box that played "Für Elise." A money gift. A decorated Christmas tree topped with an elf. Toys for Santa Anonymous. And a six-foot stuffed gorilla.

The gorilla was for my other best friend, a man named Louie. Throughout the years I'd known him, he'd joked about a monkey in Las Vegas, a monkey that talked. He said it said "Maw-Maw." I didn't believe him. But I wanted him to have the gorilla.

At the last minute, I went on a field trip with Shane and his classmates. He asked me the day before, said I hadn't been on one for a long time. His voice had that tone to it, that I-mean-business tone.

I rode with the bus of sixth graders to the science museum. We tromped around, saw how the wind works, looked at dinosaur bones, and watched a space movie at the omnitheater. On the way home, the snow blew and swirled, almost a blizzard. Shane sat across the aisle from me. He looked at me and winked. I winked back because I knew what he meant. We talked a lot without words. I could even call him home sometimes without saying a word. That's how close we were. As though on cue, we both started singing "Jingle Bells." Then the other children joined in, until the teacher shushed us.

I found the tree that Christmas, too. The magic tree, I called it. Echo and I were walking through a store the week before Christmas when I spotted it. Iridescent needles, the color of pearls, glowed softly with pink lights. Someone had decorated it with beads, crystals, hearts, and life-sized white feathered birds. A train chugged and whistled around the base of the tree. It was so pretty I stood and stared.

"Why don't you get it?" Echo said.

"No," I said. "It's artificial. The children won't like that. Besides, it's too expensive."

The next day I drove back to the store.

"I'll take that tree," I told the clerk. "And everything on it."

I stayed up late that night. When all the ornaments were in place, I plugged in the lights and called the children. The train chugged around the bottom. An angel sat on top.

"Not bad for a fake tree," Shane said.

"It's pretty, Mom. Real pretty," said Nichole.

It took my breath away, as it had in the store.

Magic was in the air that Christmas. We all felt it. Didn't know where it came from or what it meant. But it was there. It felt the way you think every Christmas will feel when you're a kid.

Except for the snow globe.

Some of Nichole's friends were over that day baking Christmas cookies when Joey stopped by to bring us her gifts. Family gifts, she called them.

"Sorry," she said, handing me a package. "The dog ate your other one. Norwegian *lefse* bread," she explained. "It was on the table."

I opened the box and took out a snow globe. This one had a family in it, a mother with her little girl and boy, standing in the snow singing carols.

Shane turned the snow globe upside down, shook it, then set it on the table and watched the snow fall.

"My turn," said Nichole.

The next moment, the snow globe crashed to the floor.

We cleaned up the mess. No one got cut. But something about it made me feel uneasy. I shook the feeling off.

Christmas Eve we went to midnight church service together. I cried during "Silent Night" like I usually do. At the end of the service I put an arm around each of the children and pulled them in close. I felt blessed. It felt like life was finally coming around and God was on our side.

The struggle seemed worth it.

This year, this Christmas, had been the best of our lives. Pieces were missing, but more was in place this year than wasn't. I sensed but hadn't learned the truth yet: each moment in time we have it all, even when we think we don't. We stepped out of the church into the cool starry night, a mother and her two children, and moved toward a future already foretold.

# Three

"I don't know what's coming next," I said to my friend. "I don't know what my future holds."

"Don't worry," she said. "Your soul does."

G UESS WHAT WE DID AT SCHOOL TODAY?"
Nichole says.

"What?" I ask.

"We had to describe our dream home. Everybody else wanted a big, expensive mansion. Then I told them about my dream home—a small yellow cottage in the Virgin Islands."

It's funny how our dreams change with time.

. . . . . . .

It was January of 1991. Life looked good. The children were doing well, although Shane seemed a little withdrawn. We had plans to move to a new home, our dream home, if I could negotiate the deal. But I started crying and couldn't stop. There was no explanation, no obvious cause for my grief. That's why I couldn't understand it. I wasn't the kind of woman who cried. Not much. Not much at all. There hadn't been time.

Dreams die hard.

My dream of what marriage would be like had died hard—a long, drawn-out, malnourished death.

Don't get me wrong; we were meant to be together. But it wasn't meant to last. The marriage didn't bring the happiness, joy, or fulfillment I had hoped it would. Instead it made me cold, afraid, and angry. Almost bitter. I kept trying harder and harder, at first biting my tongue, then trying to nag the marriage into becoming what I thought it should be.

Neither approach worked.

I didn't know much about being a woman then. Didn't know much about being a person. I was scared and didn't know that either.

One night, in the middle of the night, I found my soul. I came to suddenly, but I wasn't in bed. I was up on the ceiling looking down.

I studied a woman lying on the bed. Then I realized the woman was me. I look so different than I look in the mirror, I thought. The next instant I was back in my body. Some people might scoff, call it a dream. But I know the difference between dreaming and wakefulness. I didn't know then what the experience meant, but I know now. I was more than a physical mass. I had a soul. In my late twenties, I began to awaken to it.

Much of my life I had spent time out of my body, but in a different way. I had learned to ignore myself. I had abandoned myself—the way you do when you think who you are, what you feel, what you want is wrong.

My childhood had been long and lonely. My mother's first husband had died, leaving her to fend for herself and her children, my two half-sisters and one half-brother. That happened in the forties, when it was harder for women to be alone and make their own way. Then my father came along, sired me, and left a few years later.

The family fell apart after that. My brother and sisters left home. Mama got busy. I sat there alone, stunned, wondering where all the people had gone.

One day when I was twelve, I was so hurt and angry that I told God to go away, too. I was walking down the street on a Sunday morning. Mama had sent me to church. I looked up at the heavens and said, "God, if you are real, that makes this even worse because it means you don't love me. So I'll handle things myself from here on."

Everyone said God was love, but this didn't feel like love to me.

I remember the day Daddy called me into the bedroom to say he was going away. That's all he said: "I'm going away." Then he did. I was three, but I remember. I remember the smell of beer on his breath, too. That smell seemed part of him.

He played the piano, played with a jazz band in New Orleans. Mama said I got it from him, my music.

Daddy used to have me dance for him. He'd take me to clubs, then he'd play the piano and I'd dance on top of it. It took me a long time to learn I didn't have to dance for men unless I wanted to. It took longer to separate the smell of whiskey and beer on a man's breath from love.

The man I married had that smell on his breath. He smelled like Daddy.

The fire in the marriage lasted long enough to beget two children. Nichole was born one month before our first anniversary.

Beautiful, outspoken, solid in spirit and structure.

Two years and two months later, Shane arrived. By the time I was pregnant with him, I was out of spirit, fire, hope—all the things people need to keep going.

We lived in an old, yellow, run-down house then. It was small, with holes running clear through to the outside. It had peeling wallpaper and stained orange carpeting. I couldn't find the spark to do anything about it until I got pregnant with Shane. Then suddenly I wanted to fix that house up. I found ways, found money, and learned to do things I'd never done before: patch holes, sand floors, hang wallpaper.

I felt glad to be alive. Started thanking God for everything, even the things that hurt. By now I knew God was real. I had been talking to God again for a long time, even before I met the man I married. That helped. But being thankful helped more.

I made that house pretty, the way a woman does when she sets her mind to it. Soon I thought that old yellow house was the most beautiful home on the block.

I remembered a dream there, too. It's funny how dreams can disappear, get buried under layers of life. I had a dream when I was young. I wanted to be a writer. I knew in sixth grade that's what I wanted to do. More than anything, I wanted to write stories for a newspaper.

I held onto that dream until high school, when I forgot all my dreams. But that dream of writing came back. One day I was painting a room, an alcove off the bedroom, when I remembered it. It rose as clear as a morning sunrise and stuck there, the way a thing does when we're supposed to see it.

I looked up at the ceiling and said, "God, if I'm supposed to be a writer, you're going to have to show me."

Before sunset the next day, I had my first journalism job, writing stories for a community newspaper.

I made five dollars for my first story. The money counted because it made me feel professional. But the thrill came when I saw my byline on the front page of the paper. I slept hugging that paper. Then to top it off, someone wrote a letter to the editor saying what a good job I had done.

I didn't know yet about universal love. I thought everything was a coincidence.

I refurbished the little yellow house. Began a career I loved. And on January 30, 1979, Shane Anthony Beattie came into this world. I worried before he was born if I'd be able to love him as much as I loved Nichole. That worry was needless. I adored them both.

I spent the first year of Shane's life holding him. Just holding him close to me. I knew he was my last child. I wanted to relish every moment with him. I was young then but already knew how fast time passed.

Nichole had some reservations about Shane at first. I'd be vacuuming, and she'd tug on my shirt. "Mom," she'd say, "the baby's crying."

"What's wrong?" I'd ask.

"I pinched him," she'd say.

We worked it out, though. The three of us always found a way to work things out. I stayed in that marriage for ten years, long after it and my dreams about it had died. Spent years working at understanding what it meant to love myself, what it meant to have my own soul, what it meant to awaken to myself.

My writing career grew, too. In 1985 a publisher commissioned me to write a book about what I'd learned about loving myself. Soon after I signed that contract, I ended my marriage. I couldn't tell people they could honor their hearts and souls if I wasn't doing that.

I was learning I didn't write to teach others; I wrote to teach myself. And the two were really the same.

When we got the divorce, I told him. I said it loud and clear: I get these babies. You can visit. You can call. They can go with you because you're their daddy. No matter what else happens, you'll always be their daddy. But I get these kids. And don't ever try to take them away from me.

He said he wouldn't.

I had already given up one child, a son, when I was younger. He came in those dark years, the years when I didn't talk to God. I wasn't going to do that again, lose another child.

I told the judge: Don't worry about support. I'll handle things. Let me have my babies and I'll take care of them fine on my own.

Which I did.

But losing the dream of a traditional family broke my heart. It broke Shane's, too. He got quiet for almost a year after his daddy left. I talked to him as much as I could, tried to help him, but he was working it out the only way he knew.

And then one day he snapped out of it. Almost in a moment it seemed his heart had healed.

I pulled him aside after his daddy left and talked straight to him. "Just because your father's gone, you are not the man of the house," I said. "Your only job is to be a kid. Do you understand that?"

He said he did. But he still got protective about our family, the way men do.

Dreams may die hard, but new ones come along, too. Over time our family healed. As the eighties came to a close, we regrouped. Our lives went in a new direction. We began to understand that the three of us were a real family.

Sometimes I worried because Shane didn't have a man around all the time. He had his best friend, John. And this past year his dad had moved back to town. Seeing each other more made both of them happy. He loved his daddy. He liked Nichole's friends, the Get Along Gang. But he especially liked Ray.

They came softly into our lives, the Get Along Gang, floating in from nowhere the way people do. Then they stuck, like gnats on flypaper. Every time I turned around, one or more of them was there. They'd been friends since junior high. Nichole borrowed the name from Saturday morning cartoons. She said it fit because they helped each other get along.

Joey, blond with a high-pitched giggle. Every night after school she sat at the kitchen table with Nichole, scratching out algebra problems, laughing so hard I often had to shush her.

She talked to me a lot, wondering when she'd meet her true love. I told her the same thing I told myself. "It'll come, honey," I said. "But in its own time."

Ingrid was quiet, feminine, but behind

her shyness there were sparks in her eyes.

Tall, beautiful, and outspoken, that was Carmen. She played the piano, sang, and loved to bake. Whenever I smelled caramel rolls, I knew Carmen was there.

Then along came Ray. Small, but lithe, a natural athlete and the only boy in the Get Along Gang. I didn't pay much attention to him at first, didn't like the idea of boys hanging around. But he stopped me in my tracks one day.

"Mrs. Beattie," he said, "we need to talk. I get the feeling you don't like me much, and I think we should sit down and work this out."

So we did.

Ray was young. Said he wanted only two things. He wanted to be the best football player ever for the Ponies, the high school football team. And he wanted to go to college someday. Didn't know where the money would come from, though.

It wasn't long before he started calling me mom, his second mom.

Ray was the man in Shane's life, besides Shane's daddy. Ray showed him things, helped him learn things. Ray didn't mind.

He liked being looked up to. He liked Shane. Most people did. Oh, Shane could be a pistol, no doubt about that. But there was something about him that won your heart, right from the start.

Shane was a natural at being a kid. I asked him once, in all my grown-up fluff, to teach me how to do that. Show me how to be a kid, I said. We were walking along the dock at the river. He looked at me, grinned, pushed me in the water, then jumped in after me.

"That's how!" he said. "You just jump in!"

The trip to the Virgin Islands was Shane's idea. He started it. He started a lot of things in our family. Nestled up to me one day and pointed to an ad, a two-page spread of the Virgin Islands, in a copy of *Reader's Digest.*

"Can we go there, Mom?" he asked.

I was a soft touch for Shane. Had been since he was born. Sometimes Nichole sent him to do the front-line work for her, the way kids do.

"Sure, baby," I said. "We can go there."

The summer of 1990 we did go there. Rented a castle by the sea on the island of St. Thomas. We left the airport and drove on the left-hand side of the road until we pulled up to a cabanalike front with a placard bearing the name "The Place" over the door.

I thought it looked small and plain until we walked down the winding stairway and stood in the middle of a tropical courtyard complete with palm trees, orange and pink hibiscus flowers, a lit fountain with tadpoles, a swimming pool, and an iguana.

Rooms surrounded the courtyard. In back, a long stairway led to a private beach with a dock and a gazebo stretched out over the Caribbean.

It was nighttime, but I was sure the water looked as turquoise as it had in the ad.

We found a feeling there, a feeling different from anything we'd known. It was slow, sultry, relaxed. That trip and that vacation house inspired my decision to move. We were going to buy our dream house.

The idea got clear toward the end of 1990. In December I found the house, but I was hesitant at first. I shook my head and said no, it's too big, too expensive.

I thought about it into January. When I got over being afraid, I saw that it was everything we wanted. It had enough rooms so the children could have their own floor, and I could have my writing offices and bedroom on a separate floor. It had a yard big enough for a swimming pool, something Shane and Nichole had pestered me about. Room for a pool table, something else Shane wanted. And he'd finally get a bedroom as big as his sister's.

It would mean moving to Minneapolis from our place in Stillwater. I was concerned about upsetting the children's routines, but I spent so much time in the car driving back and forth, I decided it would be better for us all.

I knew it was time to move. I could feel it. And the feeling wouldn't let me go.

Time was flying by. In four years, Nichole would be leaving for college. This house would be the perfect place to celebrate these last years of living together.

The children looked at the house. They liked it. I began negotiations but didn't talk about it much. I didn't want to get their hopes up until I knew we had a deal.

January 30 was Shane's twelfth birthday. We had a tradition, the children and I. On birthday night the person who had the birthday got to choose the dinner arrangements—favorite home-cooked meal or favorite restaurant. The children had learned that it was smarter to go the restaurant route. The demands of single parenthood and a career had shoved my cooking skills aside. Once when scolding Nichole about table manners, I had asked her what she'd been taught about etiquette. "This is what I learned," she had said. "Throw away the wrappers when you're done."

This year, for his birthday, Shane wanted to go to Red Lobster to celebrate. Shane brought his best friend, John, with him. Nichole brought Joey. Shane ordered crab legs. At age twelve, even earlier, he enjoyed cracking his way through a plate of legs.

The waiters sang "Happy Birthday." It embarrassed him, but he liked it. I could tell.

We talked about goals and dreams for the next year, toasted the wonder years, then made a pact. No matter how old we were or where we lived, we'd always get together on our birthdays. For dinner. For love. Forever.

We made another pact, too. We agreed that whether we had many lifetimes or one, we'd always be together as a family.

I asked Shane where he'd like to go this year, whether he had any ideas for vacations or trips. He thought about it for a while, then shrugged his shoulders.

"I think you've taken me everywhere I've wanted to go, Mom," he said.

Nichole apologized because she didn't have a gift for Shane. "How about this?" she said. "You can come skiing with Joey and me this Saturday."

Shane's eyes lit up. He said that would be great.

At home later that evening, Shane sidled up to me while I sat at my dressing table brushing my hair. He opened my jewelry drawer and took out a small gold cross, one his father had given me at the time of our divorce.

"Can I have this?" he asked.

"Don't be silly," I said. I thought he was teasing.

Shane took a deep breath and repeated his question. "Mom, can I have this?"

His tone caught my attention. I knew he was serious.

"Sure, honey," I said. "You can have that."

The following day was the Friday before the birthday ski trip. Shane stopped me in the kitchen, pulled down his sweater neck, and pointed to the cross. It was hanging on a gold chain around his neck.

"God is with me now," he said quietly.

I made myself a cup of tea, studying a note on the kitchen table. It was from my mother. She had stopped by earlier this week, before leaving town on a vacation. She wanted me to have her out-of-town phone number in case of emergency.

She never did that.

A few minutes after Shane went to bed, I followed him to his bedroom. That's when I told him I had made a deal on the house. We were going to move. It was settled today. It would be everything he ever wanted— swimming pool, pool table, big bedroom. His eyes got wide and he smiled.

I felt so happy to be able to do this for him. For his sister. For us.

"Let's do prayers," I said.

It was a simple prayer. We closed our eyes, held hands, and thanked God for our family.

I kissed him good-night and turned out the light. Tomorrow was a big day.

I had a hard time falling asleep that night. The clock said four A.M. the last time I noticed.

It wasn't, as the song says, that I thought we'd get to see forever. But I thought we'd have more time than we did. I didn't know the end was coming, not that soon.

Now I know why I was crying all month. We were saying good-bye.

# Four

We were driving through the buttes in Utah when he pointed out the window.

"See that? It's a precipice."

"I know," I said. "I fell off one once."

I'M WORKING IN MY OFFICE, A SIMPLE ROOM decorated with pictures from *Robin Hood, Avalon, Treasure Island,* and *Curious George.* My friend Bobby calls to visit. He works with grieving people, people with broken hearts. We talk about how much it hurts to lose people, especially when someone is ripped from your life in a moment.

He tells a story about the time a woman ended her relationship with him suddenly, unexpectedly. "It was a smaller loss, in the scale of things," he says. "But I didn't see it coming. I had to go to work, give a speech that day. Didn't know how I'd do it. It felt like someone had ripped my heart out of my chest and I couldn't breathe."

"I know what you mean," I say. "I felt that way for two years."

. . . . . . .

Shane woke me up at seven on Saturday morning.

"I've got a game at eight," he said. "I can't be late. Mom, come with," he begged. "You haven't been to any of my

57

basketball games this year."

I was tired. I had slept only three hours. But his voice had that tone to it again. Shane was a natural athlete, good at any sport with a ball. He played football, baseball, hockey, basketball, soccer. He ice-skated, roller-skated, and studied karate. I liked going to his practices and games, but I couldn't attend all of them. This morning I knew it was time to go.

I dragged myself out of bed and went to the school gymnasium with him. He was so sweet, setting up a chair for me on the sidelines, walking over, and patting my head during time-outs. I watched him with mother's pride. All the kids are great, I thought. But mine's special. Even with uniforms and at a distance, I could tell Shane. I could feel his energy. He had a walk, a distinct stride. So mature, yet still a little boy. God, I love him, I thought. I'm so glad to be his mother.

I didn't understand a lot about basketball—or any sport for that matter—but I watched with interest and some understanding. I wasn't athletic. Had never played any sport or done any physical activity other than walking, jogging, and occasionally jumping into a swimming pool. But I knew enough to know Shane was good.

He played hard that morning, but his timing was off. Made a lot of shots, but no baskets. His team lost the game by one point.

On the way home he insisted that we stop for breakfast. He ordered strawberry pancakes, his favorite.

I can't recall what I ate.

"You played good," I said. "I'm proud of you. But you didn't shoot worth a dang."

He agreed.

We went home to meet Christie, our housekeeper and nanny. She planned to take Nichole, Shane, and Joey to the slopes. Joey's mother would drive them home. The drive took about twenty-five minutes, longer if the roads were bad, so we often carpooled.

I didn't understand a lot about skiing. But many of the children and adults in the surrounding communities skied. It scared me. I pictured breaking my leg if I tried. But the kids took to it like frogs to a lily pond. They loved it. And this morning they were excited about spending the day at the slopes.

When Christie rang the doorbell, Nichole rushed in and kissed me good-bye. Shane followed. I gave them money for admission and Shane money for ski rental. Nichole had her own skis; she got them for a Christmas present. Although I had recently bought Shane a new ski jacket and pants, I didn't want to buy him skis yet.

"Be home by six," I yelled as they walked out the door. Nichole promised they would. "I love you guys," I said. And they were gone.

It was a strange day. I felt like I was waiting for something, but I didn't know what. I had felt that way all month, maybe longer. That afternoon I turned on the television, using the remote control to click through the channels. Nothing interested me. I paused at a movie I had seen before and decided to watch it again. The movie was *Always,* a story about a pilot firefighter who dies in a plane crash. Most of the story takes place after his death, when he comes back in spirit or ghost form to help his girlfriend get on with her life.

The movie showed her struggle to care about life again after his death. It showed their struggle to let go of each other. It was poignant, and I cried watching it now, just as I had the first time.

I hadn't thought much about life after death, but the ideas that our spirits live forever, that there is more to this world than we can see, and that love is such a potent force appealed to me. I felt comforted by the idea of being vital after the death experience.

I didn't think about death much. I knew I was getting older, but I figured I had another forty years.

I had seen some tragic early deaths. A neighbor's child had committed suicide at fifteen. A child I baby-sat a few times, a twin, had drowned on a camping trip. A neighbor, a single parent, had died of cancer at age forty-five, leaving two children behind. But I didn't want to think about those deaths. I didn't want to get too close.

Death scared me.

I looked at the clock. It was eight. I wondered why the children weren't home yet. They were supposed to be back by six.

At approximately the same time the movie ended, a twelve-year-old boy finished playing a video game at the indoor recreation area at Afton Alps. He chatted with his sister for a minute. He grinned, said, "See ya," then headed for one more run on the slopes.

He talked a friend of his sister's into trying an expert hill, a hill called The Face. He had been carefully skiing beginner hills all day. Now he wanted to try one run down The Face, one run to end the day. A woman and her husband, a local couple who knew the children, waved to them as they left the chalet. The woman thought about warning them. They were heading for The Face. She shrugged it off. When kids decide to do something, there's no talking them out of it.

It was a clear, starry February night, and the hill was crowded with skiers. When the two children reached the top, the boy turned to the girl he was skiing with.

"Let's face it!" he shouted. He dug his poles into the snow and pushed off.

I was puttering around the house when the telephone rang.

"Mrs. Beattie?" a man's voice asked.

"Yes," I said.

"Your son has been injured in a ski accident. I'm with the Afton Ski Patrol," he said. "He's unconscious. But don't worry. Skiers get knocked unconscious a lot. Sometimes they're out for an hour or two. I'm sure he'll be fine. Stay where you are. We'll call you right back."

Shane had sustained minor injuries from time to time in nearly every sport he played. I hung up the phone, sure that everything would be okay. He was sturdy, strong, vital. Shane would be fine.

The boy's small form lay motionless on the slope. He had fallen going over a mogul. Stood up. Struggled to regain his balance. Another skier had come from behind, knocking him down again. This time he didn't move. The couple who had seen him leaving the chalet were riding in the ski lift. The woman looked down, saw the motionless form, and recognized him. She got off the lift and skied toward him. She was a registered nurse.

The girl he'd been skiing with reached the bottom of the hill. She looked around for her ski partner. She thought he was right behind her. She looked up. People were running toward a fallen skier. She whipped off her skis and charged up the hill.

The nurse skied down to the chalet to summon medical help. The first-aid sled arrived. Artificial respiration wasn't working. The medic administered oxygen and someone called an ambulance. "Find his sister," said the nurse. She had worked with dying people before. She knew when the life force was present in a body; she knew when it wasn't. This didn't look good. This looked as grim as anything she'd seen.

I waited by the telephone. Fifteen minutes later it rang again. "Your son's still not conscious. We're taking him to St. Paul Ramsey Hospital. Meet us there," the voice said. "But don't worry. Everything will be fine."

Be calm, I thought. Get your purse and car keys. All you have to do is drive to the hospital. Meet your son. Be by his side. Everything will be fine.

I turned on the ignition and backed out of the driveway.

A fourteen-year-old girl stood by the back of the ambulance. "Help him!" she said. "Take care of him! That's my brother!" The medics slashed off his jacket and hooked up an IV. "Has he been drinking? Taking drugs?" they asked. "Geez, no!" she screamed. "He's a twelve-year-old boy! All he's had tonight is Pepsi! Do something!" The medic started to cut off a chain that hung around his neck, a gold chain with a cross on it. "Don't touch that!" she screamed. "Leave it on him!" They closed the doors and sped toward the emergency room.

I raced toward St. Paul. Just get there, I thought. Get there. Strange, dark thoughts passed through my mind. They were morbid, different from the way I usually thought. I shook them off. I parked in the lot next to the emergency room and walked through the glass doors. A nurse met me at the entrance.

"I'm Mrs. Beattie. I'm here to see . . . "

She looked at me, she looked at me so strangely, so differently than anyone had ever looked at me before. I didn't understand the look. She took my arm and led me to a small room furnished with chairs, a phone, and a single cross on the wall.

"Do you have someone you can call?" she asked.

Those words—**Do you have someone you can call?**—broke my heart. I knew what those words meant.

I talked to a doctor. He said something about brain injury. Swelling. More tests.

For the next three days I prayed and waited for a miracle. My friends surrounded me. Twenty, thirty, or more stayed at the hospital by my side. They didn't know what to do; I didn't know what to do. What I did know was I wanted my baby. I wanted him back and unhurt. Once, I picked up a Bible in the family room, reading where it opened, hoping I'd get a message from God telling me everything would be fine. My thumb landed on the story of Jesus raising Lazarus from the dead. Maybe this is a sign, I thought. But it didn't feel like a sign. It felt like a cruel joke.

Then the doctors and nurses started saying something about no hope. Those are the words I remember: **No hope.** I brought in additional expert medical help, healers, and ministers. They all looked at me, shook their heads, and said, "Sorry, no hope."

Well, do you know what I told those people?

I bucked up like a mule and said, "No! Don't you ever tell me that. Don't you ever say there's no hope. I've spent my whole life believing there's hope. And there always is. So don't tell me that now. Not about my baby."

Sometimes I couldn't bear to be in Shane's room. I felt like I was going to explode, go insane. The respirator whooshed as it pushed air into his lungs. He was hooked to needles, monitors, tubes. I held his hand around the needles, gently squeezing his fingers, but he didn't squeeze back. I'd go sit with my friends for a while, then go back into his room.

I remembered a time from a few weeks back.

"Let's go sledding," he had said.

"I'm too old," I'd said.

"No, you're not," he said.

"It's too cold," I said.

"Put on snow pants," he said. "Let's go."

So we did. We took his sled to a hill across the street. After ten runs down the hill I was tired.

"You go alone for a while," I said. "I'll watch."

He climbed to the top of the hill, then slid to the bottom. But instead of slowing to a stop in the open area, he veered to the right, slammed into a tree, and rolled off the sled. He lay there on his back in the snow.

I yelled, "Shane, are you all right?" He didn't answer, but I knew he was teasing. I ran over to him. "Stop it," I said. "You're not funny."

He sat up quickly, smiled, and said, "Psych!"

"Don't tease like that," I said. "If anything

happened to you, I don't know what I'd do. I don't think I could go on. Do you understand that?" I asked.

He looked at me, got real serious, and said yes, he knew that.

Now, I kept wishing he'd sit up, smile, and say "psych." He didn't.

. . . . . . .

On the third day, the doctors told me that in three hours they had to turn off the life-support equipment. Shane's kidneys had shut down, his body wasn't working, he was brain-dead. It was time. Medically, there were no more options.

I was standing in a hallway when they told me this. I'd been stunned but fairly calm, given the circumstances. But now I started screaming at the doctor. "Damn it," I told her, "this is my baby you're talking about!" Then I kicked the metal door across from me. Reared back and slammed my foot into it as hard as I could.

Echo was standing next to me. She got scared when she saw me kick that door.

She grabbed my hand and started to drag me away.

"Don't worry," she told the doctor. "She always comes around and does what she needs to do, does the right thing. She always handles things. She'll be okay."

I wasn't so sure. What was doing the right thing? Letting your baby die? Making funeral arrangements? That's the right thing? How can you do the right thing when the right thing isn't happening?

Another doctor handed me a pill, an antianxiety drug. I swallowed it. Then Echo and I went into the bathroom and sat on the floor. I knew she was right. I had to get it together and do whatever needed to be done. Echo said we'd get through this one step at a time. I swallowed hard and pushed the rage away. The pill began to take effect. I started to calm down.

Shane's friends, Nichole's friends, and family members said their good-byes. Then I entered his room.

I cut off a lock of Shane's hair. I touched his foot. I had always loved his little feet. And I held him while they shut off the respirator.

"I love you," I said. "I always have. I always will."

The second they turned off the machine, he stopped breathing. A whiff of air escaped from his lungs, and he didn't move again. I knew then he hadn't been breathing, hadn't been alive for days. The machines had just made it look that way.

The room got quiet. A nurse began unhooking the tubes and needles. Echo looked nervous, then started to walk out of the room. I stood there. Echo looked at me. The nurse looked at me. The clock ticked. I looked at Shane. And I stood there. I couldn't move. Finally, I put one foot in front of the other, put one foot in front of the other because that's the only way to walk away, and I walked out of that room and out of the hospital.

And it was the hardest thing I have ever done in my life.

．．．．．．．

I held up pretty well that week, the funeral week. Nichole and I and the people who had flown in from out of town stayed at a hotel near the hospital. I wasn't ready to go home yet.

Once, I lost my way in the hotel hallways. I was going from one room to another and I got confused and felt crazy and didn't know where to go or how to get there. I sat down on the floor and cried. I wanted someone to find me and help me. Nobody did. After a while, I got up. I found my way to the lobby and asked how to get to my room.

Something strange had happened to my mind. It didn't work well. I couldn't reason things out, think my way through, as I had in the past. I was in a new world now, and I could already see I'd have to get through another way.

I didn't like it.

Hundreds of people attended the wake and funeral. It helped that so many people cared. I felt stronger when people were around, although I didn't have much to say. Sometimes I couldn't remember or recognize people I knew well. I'd have a vague memory that I knew someone, but I'd have to hear a name repeated before it registered. It felt strange watching these people from so many parts of my life file by. Each one has helped me learn some kind of lesson, I thought. I hadn't always liked what I was learning, but each lesson, each time in my life, had been important. Even now I could sense that, as out of my mind as I was. And I might not have looked it, but I was out of my mind.

My father came to the wake. He stayed for five minutes, said he was sorry Shane died. This was the first time he'd met the children. We both felt awkward, but I admired him for coming. It took courage.

My brother, sisters, and mother hadn't been together in one room for years until now. The day after Shane got hurt I asked each one to put aside differences and help me get through this because I needed them. They agreed. I thought it was good and loving of them to do that.

My brother and I hugged for the first time in our lives. He told me he loved me, and I said I loved him too.

I read two poems at Shane's funeral. One talked about a mother being willing to love a child, experience all those joys, even if she must live to grieve his passing. The other was a simple message. It talked about two important things you could give a child, roots and wings. I said I gave Shane roots. Now it was time for me to give him wings. Shane's best friend, John, said a couple sentences. Then Louie talked about how there were only two things: fear and love. Whatever isn't love is fear, he said. Whatever isn't fear is love.

I set out all Shane's sports equipment at the funeral, hockey stick, football helmet, basketball, football—his favorite things. When the service ended, I got up and began gathering everything together. The funeral director said I didn't have to do that. I said yes, I did. I was his mother, and this was the last motherly job I'd get to do. I've taken care of this baby all his life, and I will do it now, too.

After the service we went outside. Louie had arranged for a hot-air balloon to be tied on the funeral grounds. It couldn't soar freely because the cemetery was close to the airport and in a flight path. But it hovered and hissed nearby. Each of us held a balloon, all different colors. And all together, we let go.

When the children were little, they loved balloons. When one of their balloons would fly into the air, I comforted them by saying, "That's okay. God catches all your balloons. And first thing when you get to heaven, you get a big bouquet of every balloon you've ever lost. So don't cry. They'll all be there waiting for you."

The weather was unusually warm and sunny for a February day in Minnesota. The sky was clear, not an airplane in sight, as hundreds of balloons sailed up, up, and away, beyond where we could see.

I let go of my balloon last, so it trailed behind. But even that one eventually disappeared, too.

I didn't eat at the reception. People said I should, but food tasted like dried paper and it was hard to swallow. People's faces looked funny, as though I were seeing them through a distortion lens.

That night a small group of us went to a comedy club in St. Paul. Louie had arranged to do a special show. The club was small. I laughed a little, listened as much as I could. At the end, he looked up at the ceiling, blew a kiss into the air, and said, "Shane, we love you."

And it was over.

Our friends went back to their lives, and Nichole and I returned to Stillwater. The house looked different, felt different without Shane. Like the snow globe, my world had shattered, and I couldn't put the pieces back together. I was shattered, too, broken in a way I had never been before. I sat on Shane's bed and looked around. Looming ahead were endless days of pain and missing him.

I don't want to go through this, I thought. God, I don't want to go through this.

I had fallen off a cliff. Or maybe I was pushed. I felt lost, confused, and alone, like I had in the hotel hallway. It would take months and months before I could hear or believe what was whispered to me that night, whispered to my heart by the angels. It would be longer before I cared.

**You have begun a journey into the unknown. Although you may think you have been abandoned, remember: You are never alone.**

# Part II

# Five

"The lesson is ancient and tragic,"
he whispered, holding me close.
"The young prince is dead.
And darkness descends upon
the land."

WHEN I FINISH THE LAST CHAPTER, A HURricane washes through me. My hands shake. My body shakes. I leave the computer for days, striving to regain balance. There is a connective thread that turns isolated incidents into a story, random hours and days into a life, one with meaning. Shane's death breaks that thread in my life and in the story. Upon finding the slender ends of that thread, I return to the computer, bringing with me a gift from Echo, a white porcelain angel to keep on my desk as I write, a reminder that I'm not alone.

I stare at the angel, remembering how much I appreciate Echo's love. I pick up the phone.

"Just called to say I love you," I say when she answers.

"That's funny," she says. "I was thinking about calling you and saying the same thing. I guess we're on track."

The challenge is no longer to hold up, as it's been for so many years. The lesson now is about opening up.

. . . . . . .

I sat on the cliffs at Maui, watching the waves crash against the rocky shore fifteen hundred feet below. Whales surfaced, then disappeared into the ocean. The sun shone brightly in the sky that day, the first clear day in the week since I'd come to Hawaii.

It was a strange vacation. My half-brother and half-sister had met annually in Hawaii. This year they'd invited me to join them. I had to make a decision about moving. I had signed the purchase agreement the evening before Shane's death. Now the owners of that home were pressuring me for a decision.

No course of action felt right. My life didn't feel right. I was certain a mistake had been made, a mistake I wasn't prepared to accept.

I hesitated to pull Nichole out of Stillwater, away from her school and friends, now that she had lost her brother. Yet neither she nor I was comfortable staying in that house with all its reminders of Shane's absence. The school bus that pulled up each day at three o'clock and dropped off all Shane's classmates, but not Shane. Shane's empty bedroom. His friends walking by the front window. The tennis courts where we awkwardly batted the ball around. The lake where we sat. Everything we looked at pierced our hearts, penetrated the fog, making the pain worse—if making the pain worse was possible.

We decided to move. Christie had invited Nichole to go to Bermuda for a week. My family had asked me to meet them in Hawaii, a time to become reacquainted. I arranged for the move to take place while we were gone.

There was no joy in anticipating the move. It had been six weeks since my son's death. The pain had diminished by only the most imperceptible, yet welcomed, amount. But it still felt as it did the day I walked into the emergency room, the day the nurse looked at me that way. Like someone had held a shotgun to my chest and blown a hole through my heart.

I was learning to function feeling that way. I cried when I needed to and laughed if I had the chance to do that. In some ways life had become simple. I got up each day and moved around. One day, about two weeks after Shane's death, I walked out to the kitchen.

Carmen, Ingrid, and Nichole, some of the Get Along Gang, were sitting there.

"I wrote about you in English class today," Carmen said.

"What could you possibly write about me?" I asked.

"We had to write an essay about courage," Carmen said. "I used you for my subject."

I started crying, said I didn't want to be known for my courage.

"What do you want to be known for?" Carmen asked.

The answer rolled off my tongue. "I'd like to be known for having an easy life."

Like it or not, I was already learning that in the worst and darkest times, I could find specks of light, moments of joy. What I didn't want to learn was the other, harsher lesson—that in life's brightest moments there could also be unbearable pain. I wasn't prepared to accept it, not yet. The lesson was too hard, too grown-up, too inherently cruel.

"I always want to go back to that moment in time right before an accident happens," my friend Wendy said.

"I know what you mean," I told her.

I missed Shane terribly. Missed his presence, his voice, the touch of him, the feel of him. Some nights I lay awake until the wee hours of the morning, trying to penetrate the veil that divides this world from the next. My efforts, my staring, my trying to pierce the ethers resulted only in a headache. The veil that some say is thin felt like a cement barricade to me. Shane felt far away. Gone forever.

And I had already begun to see the layering, the compounding of losses.

Ray, one of the Get Along Gang, had asked me to attend his annual wrestling banquet a few weeks after Shane's death.

"Mom," he said. "I need you there." I sat next to Ray's mother, a beautiful young woman. We proudly watched Ray and the others receive their awards. There will be no banquets with Shane, I realized suddenly. No athletic events, no graduations. All the quiet dreams I had taken for granted were gone.

The emcee concluded the presentations by thanking one of the local men who had worked with the young wrestlers, a man who was bravely, but not victoriously, battling cancer.

Do these people know, really know, that it can all be stripped from them in one moment? I wondered. Everything they've worked for? Everything they value? Do they know that even if we play by the rules, life doesn't?

Do they understand how fragile life really is?

Only weeks before Shane's death, Nichole had come home from school with a statistic. "Did you know that before the end of this school year, one child we know will die?" she had asked in her most serious tone.

I hadn't known that. And I had never dreamed that Shane and our family would become that statistic.

The invisible substance called meaning had been drained from my life, and most of what I saw now looked senseless: the striving, the hopes, the dreams. The struggles. Life didn't seem worthwhile. Trying was stupid. The force we were fighting felt overwhelming, the odds not in our favor.

Like many people, I had marked time in my life by events. Graduating from high school, getting married, having children, getting divorced. Now the mile marker for my life had become Shane's death. The problem was, it stopped marking time. Nothing worthwhile seemed to be coming next.

What kind of universe, world, God, life, would deliver a blow like this to anyone? It was senselessly tragic, and both its senselessness and cruelty had pulled the thin rug of trust out from under me, the magic carpet we sit on that allows us to ride out life's events with a modicum of belief that despite pain and disappointments things will be okay—that life makes sense and is worth living.

Divine order, the celestial calendar that ticks off the events of our lives, no longer seemed trustworthy. It felt selectively abusive. On a physical and emotional level, it left me in excruciating pain. On a spiritual level, it left me bankrupt.

Seething, white hot rage filled me about this thing called life. I didn't want to play anymore. It wasn't that I didn't believe in God. I did. That made things worse.

Yes, I got out of bed every day and moved around. I put one foot in front of the other and walked from room to room. But it wasn't because I was brave or had courage, as Carmen had suggested. When I slept, I would dream that Shane had died. When I opened my eyes, for one fleeting moment relief would flood through me as I realized I'd been dreaming. Then I'd remember. I was awake. And Shane really was dead.

I got up every day. But only to escape the terror I felt when I lay down.

Now, sitting on the cliffs at Maui, I listened to the pounding surf, crashing as ferociously as my emotions pounded away at me. Normally the timeless rhythm of the ocean soothed me, calmed me. This day it didn't touch my pain. I wanted to scream, to yell out, to demand reparation from the universe for the damage done to my son, my daughter, me. My family.

Instead, I scratched on a rock with my fingernail, staring at the whales below. I didn't feel alone with God.

I felt alone.

With all our high technology and sophistication, hearts still break. I had lost one of the two great loves of my life. And my heart was broken. When our heart is broken, we can't hear it. And when we can't hear our heart, we can't hear God.

All I could hear was my pain.

Some people say that pain is the gatekeeper to paradise.

"How do you get through it?" one man said. "You move slowly and try to get through."

I didn't think I would ever do that, get through. Didn't think I cared to. And from what I could see, I wasn't standing at the gate to paradise.

I had been flung into a dark, black sea of grief and despair, as vast as the ocean that crested and receded below me.

I remembered the message of the Runes, the smooth, small, white stones, harbingers, some say, of what our souls already know. How long ago had it been? It seemed like another lifetime; it was only three or four months ago that a friend had brought them by, encased in a velvet drawstring bag. Try it, she had said. I stuck my hand in carefully, then drew out two.

**Turn around and review your life, then**

pass through the gateway, the first said. If you draw this stone, you are about to experience a transformation. If you draw the blank Rune next, the second warned, the transformation may be so great as to include death.

I stuck my hand in the bag, retrieved a third stone, then turned it over, carefully examining both sides. It was blank.

This is nonsense, I scolded my friend. And I don't believe it anyway.

Now I believed it.

But I hadn't passed through this gateway. I had been pushed.

# Six

"How can I get there?" asked Dorothy.

"You must walk. It is a long journey, through a country that is sometimes pleasant and sometimes dark and terrible. However, I will use all the magic arts I know of to keep you from harm."

—THE WIZARD OF OZ

THE WORD HAS SEVEN LETTERS. THE CROSS-
word puzzle clue is *costliest*. Priciest? No.
Expensive? Way too long. I'm stuck. The following day I check the answer when the
paper arrives.

I should have known.

Dearest.

. . . . . . .

Nichole and I piled into the car. We had
enough luggage for two weeks. We were
headed on a three-day trip. It was a sponta-
neous vacation; we had planned it together
only a few days earlier. We'd drive from the
Twin Cities up to the north shore by Lake
Superior and stay in a cabin in the north
woods. Try to build a fire, although neither
of us knew how. Shane always built the fires.

It was more than that, though. We were
frantically, desperately trying to keep a
promise we'd made when Shane died. That
we'd regroup, become a happy family of two.

Nine months had passed since his death.
So far, that hadn't happened.

I pulled out of the driveway, glancing at the

house. It's a prison, I thought. Spacious, lots of light and windows. But still a prison.

I started to back out of the driveway.

"Just a sec," Nichole said. "My blanket's caught in the door."

I stopped the car. It took her only a second or two to open the door, pull in the blanket, and shut the door. I backed out, heading toward the freeway. Two blocks from home a car ran a stop sign, roaring through the intersection we were about to cross. It was a blind intersection, hidden by towering nineteenth-century houses, garages, and high fences. The speed limit was thirty miles an hour. I guessed the car to be going at least fifty.

"Did you see that?" Nichole asked.

"I sure did, honey," I said. "I'm still not breathing."

"But Mom," she insisted. "Did you really see it? I mean, if I hadn't stopped to take my blanket out of the door, if we hadn't taken that extra little time, we'd have been in the middle of the street when that happened."

Now I understood her meaning. "We probably would have," I said. "It's funny how things like that work out."

"Or don't," she said.

She chattered a while about the near miss. For a moment I sensed she had something more on her mind, something else to say. When I asked what was going on, she rested back in the seat and pulled the blanket around her.

"I want to sleep now," she said.

I didn't push it. I knew better.

I looked at her cuddled up against the door. She looked pale and drawn. She had started to complain about not feeling well when she woke up this morning, but she reassured me she'd pull out of it, be fine. I wondered.

"Are you sure you want to do this, honey?" I asked.

"We're going, Mom. We're going to have a vacation together. Keep driving," she mumbled from under the covers.

I pulled onto the freeway, heading north. It was a cold fall day. The sky was gray, and it had been for a long time. The last sunny day in Minnesota I remembered was the day of Shane's funeral.

I enjoyed the feeling of driving somewhere, having a goal, something I could do. The past months had been long and hard. I was watching my life slip away in that house, watching my life and my dreams go down the drain like cold water running out of a tub.

I squandered my savings, didn't care about money. Not anymore. I made bad decisions, personally and professionally. I was too vulnerable, too needy, too emotional. I hated that, but I couldn't help it.

I couldn't work, couldn't think clearly anymore, not the way I needed to in order to write. Instead I built a shrine in what was supposed to be my office, surrounding myself with mementos of days past, souvenirs of the three of us. Pictures of vacations. Shane's toys. A lock of his hair, the one I clipped at the hospital.

One project came across my desk that I decided to accept. A publisher asked me to edit a small manual on reasons to live when ending your own life seems like the thing to do. A book on not quitting, Scotty later called it. This was something I knew, little things to do to keep you going.

For a while I had clung to my notions of turning this house into our dream home. I'd met with the remodelers, discussed plans for changes.

None of that had come to pass. I knew when we moved in that this house wasn't going to work, not the way I wanted it to. I wasn't prepared to accept it. Wasn't prepared to lose all the dreams entangled in it. So I pretended. The truth was, I didn't know where to go next or what to do. It was still all I could do to grind through each day. I was stuck there for now.

Time passed strangely in that house, in my life, both in the remembering, as I sped down the highway, and in the living out. Sometimes one day felt three or four days long. Other times I'd look at the calendar and be surprised to see a month or two had passed.

Sometimes I didn't know if I was awake or dreaming. Maybe I was in a bad accident, I'd think. And I'm really in a coma, dreaming this. I'm going to wake up and everything will be fine, the way it used to be. Or, I'm just dreaming, I'd think. This whole thing is a long, terrible dream meant to teach me something important, and I'm going to wake up and laugh, tell people what a wretched nightmare I had. I wanted so badly for that to be true. I found the roots to the old saying about pinching yourself to see if you're real. Many times I pinched myself, and even when the pinch hurt, I still wasn't convinced.

Louie still called every morning. But most of the friends who had gathered around me in the beginning were now gone. Years later I was walking down a winding path in Laguna Beach alongside the ocean. It was a California winter day. Fresh roses bloomed. The temperature was about sixty-five degrees. I smiled at people as they passed by. When no one responded, I turned to Scotty. "People here sure are unfriendly. No one even smiles at me," I said. He looked at me. After taking a few steps, I remembered. I was wearing the purple T-shirt Louie had given me, the one with big white letters that said "Leave Me Alone."

That's what it was like now. Those who hadn't left, I had pushed away. How many times, how many days in a row, can you answer the question "How are you?" with "Not good." My friends were tired of it. I was tired of it. Even Echo and I had argued, hadn't spoken since June.

At least the looters had left, too, the looters who appear after any kind of disaster. That was a relief. My neediness and vulnerability had attracted people unconcerned with my best interests, people who wanted me to sign on the dotted line, write a check, trust them. My ability to fend them off had diminished because I no longer trusted myself. Or cared. And the empty spot in my heart wasn't yet selective about who or what it drew in to fill it up. I didn't have the strength, vitality, or discernment to stand up for myself. When I realized I couldn't trust my judgment, I pushed almost everyone away, those who loved me along with the looters.

I didn't talk to God much anymore, as I had done most of my life. What would I say? Hadn't divine providence allowed this to happen? How could I ask the same force that allowed this to happen to help me heal? Why would I want to? I was in a cold war with God.

My life had slowed almost to a stop.

I was angry with myself for not doing better, not handling my grief better. I tried my best. Therapy. Massage. Groups, when I could stand being around people. Walks. Those things may have kept me alive, but nothing made my pain go away. Nothing made me care about life again. I didn't know what else to do. My therapist had suggested an exercise: walk around the house blindfolded for two hours. I had stumbled from room to room, unsure of what I'd bump into, where my foot would land, or what might grab me next. That's how I felt most of the time, now—blindfolded, without footing, and terrified.

A few years later I would hear this story. A man went to Istanbul, his first visit there. On his way to a business meeting, this man lost his way. He began raging at himself for getting lost, until a realization allowed him to transcend his ire.

"How can I be lost? I've never been here before."

I was in a foreign country, trying to find my way around. It was a world of feelings, and I couldn't think my way through. I didn't understand this world, but I was beginning to see one thing. At least for now, I was allowed to cling tightly to no one.

Over time I had taken to doing the crossword puzzle in the daily paper, something I had never done before. At first I couldn't get one single word. Then gradually I caught on.

One day, after finishing an entire Sunday puzzle, I let out a whoop. Nichole came running into the room, asking what was wrong. "I did it!" I said. "I did the whole thing!"

It was six o'clock in the evening. I was still in my pajamas. Nichole looked at me, said she thought I was deteriorating, and suggested I get a life.

"I have one," I said. "It's just not a very good one right now."

I liked doing the puzzles. They gave me a chance to use my mind, to think at least a little bit.

Slowly I began to see a rhythm to the puzzles. If I tried too hard, strained too hard, I couldn't get it. I had to relax, let the answers come gently. So it was with the new rhythm developing in my life.

One day after finishing the crossword puzzle, I had the strangest sense. I could almost feel Shane standing next to me. Felt him standing there so strong I started crying, as if we were having a reunion. I remembered that he had been obsessed with crosswords since he was old enough to spell. I wondered. Is this where this new desire came from?

No, I thought. This is nuts. Way too mystical for me. Just the facts, please.

I read the obituaries each day, something else I'd never done before. I learned something I hadn't wanted to look at too closely before: each day, every day, people of all ages die from a variety of causes. Some people said I got morbid. I don't think so. I was learning about death. It made me sad when young people or babies died, made me sad for their parents and family. I was surprised at the number of people in their thirties and forties who died every day, people supposedly in the prime of their lives who left families and loved ones behind.

And I noticed some people lived to be more than one hundred years old.

A life span is a strange thing, I thought.

Music helped. Music sometimes helped more than talking. Sometimes I'd listen to the same songs over and over, letting the music take me and my emotions somewhere else. Nichole would become irritated with me.

"You've listened to that song four hundred times," she'd say. "I'm sick of it."

Then she'd sit by me and listen to it, too.

Sometimes we'd sit at the piano and play and sing together.

When the night has come and the land is dark
And the moon is the only light we'll see,
No, I won't be afraid, no I won't be afraid
Just as long as you stand, stand by me.

Occasionally, we'd cry together. But she hated my pain, hated it ferociously.

It was hard for me to admit as I looked at Nichole sleeping in the seat next to me, but I was losing her, too. We had begun arguing a lot lately, almost any time we were in a room together. She skipped school frequently and refused to do any homework. She was failing or barely passing most of her classes. And I didn't like the new crowd of friends she ran with. These kids weren't like the Get Along Gang. They were surly, sometimes downright rude to me. I'd tried forbidding her to see them anymore, but that hadn't worked.

Life hadn't played by the rules, so why should we? What good did it do?

Each of us was adrift in our own cold dark sea, unable to help each other, unable to do much but swim for our lives. Sometimes we'd bob to the surface, reach out, touch each other's hand, say I love you. That's what this car trip was about.

I was angry, furious, that Nichole had to go through this pain. I was mad that I had to as well.

Good will come of this someday, friends had weakly suggested. What? I wondered. You will learn things, they said. What? I wondered.

Compassion, maybe. I could see waves of it flooding over me. A new sense of being unwilling to judge others for what they did or how they did it.

A new respect for people's pain. Yes, I had that.

I could see, at a distance, that new cycles were slowly beginning in my life. Louie had sent Ahmos, his manager, into my life to help pick up the pieces of my shattered career and finances.

Ahmos couldn't do much without my cooperation, though. And I didn't care about work.

We pulled into the town of Duluth. I stopped for gas. Nichole woke up. She was sicker now. I felt her forehead; it burned to the touch. I checked the map. We were three hours from home, an hour from our destination. I'd drive there and take her to an emergency room. It seemed to me she needed antibiotics.

I drove along the dark, winding road around the western edge of Lake Superior. A fog had settled in. Nichole had fallen back to sleep. I didn't want to turn the radio on and disturb her. I started singing quietly, as softly as I could, songs from my past: "Kumbayah, my Lord, kumbayah"; "East side, west side, all around the town"; "Amazing grace, how sweet the sound."

I pulled into the emergency room parking

lot. Time had passed quickly. The doctor cultured her for strep throat. As she lay there on the examining table, she reached out and touched my hand.

"Mama, some people think things like this get better with time. What they don't know is that in some ways it gets worse. I miss Shane more every day he's gone."

After Nichole got her prescription for strep, we went to the cabin. We slept for a few hours, but we both wanted to go home. Our trip wasn't a success, but we had tried. When we pulled into the driveway in Minneapolis, I pointed to the backyard.

"Look," I said. "Have you ever seen anything like it before?"

The yard was filled with shiny blue-black ravens. Hundreds of them.

"What do you suppose it means?" I asked Nichole.

"That we're going to get our eyes pecked out?" Nichole asked.

"No," I replied, "in the medicine cards, ravens mean something. I can't remember what it is."

"Mom, you're weird," she said.

After we unpacked I searched the library for my book on the medicine cards. I looked up ravens. Going deeper into the void, it said, to learn more about life's magic.

There were two things I didn't understand. How I could go any deeper into the void. And how life could ever be magical again.

Later that evening Nichole snuggled up to me. "Mama, it was so pretty when you were singing in the car. I really liked that." I looked at her and smiled fondly. I thought she was sleeping. I didn't know she could hear me.

# Seven

Your fight is just beginning. Sometimes no one will want to hear what you're going through. You are going to have to learn to carry a great burden and most of your learning will be done alone. Don't feel frightened when they leave you. I'm sure you will come through it all okay.

—RON KOVIC,
*BORN ON THE FOURTH OF JULY*

I LIE ON THE MASSAGE TABLE, LISTENING TO public radio humming in the background. Christopher checks pulse lines in both my wrists with the finesse of a concert violinist playing a Stradivarius. He's an American practicing traditional Chinese medicine, the ancient art of acupuncture. The delicate needles gently pierce my skin as he plays connect-the-dots with ch'i, the vital energy permeating, the Chinese say, all matter, animate or not. I have not been animate for some time.

When he finishes I drive to Fremont Avenue and park in front of the house. I sit, idling, no desire to get out and go in. It is winter solstice, the day when darkness lasts its longest. The day before light begins its gradual, yet inevitable, return.

That house was the winter solstice of my life.

. . . . . . .

I sat in the Chicago airport waiting to change planes on my way back to Minneapolis. Two days until Christmas. I had done some limited publicity for the book I edited, the book on not quitting. I felt frustrated doing it, though. Most people didn't get it, quitting. They thought you had to be slashing at your wrists with a razor to quit. Yes, that was quitting. But there was another kind, a passive quitting that ran deeper. And you didn't have to do anything to yourself. Not when you quit by giving up.

I had felt agitated on the plane from West Virginia. I'd attributed it to flying and publicity. Now, as I sat waiting for my flight, I knew it was something else. I watched people sitting in the waiting area, reading, chatting, going on with their lives. I watched people tromp down the gateways, some scurrying, some shuffling. I watched life going on without me.

From nowhere a cold rage erupted. I wanted to pick up a chair and hurl it through the plate glass window. No, a row of chairs. The rage felt powerful enough, uncaring enough, to propel me into that. Is this how people feel when they go berserk? I wondered. Is this how snipers feel? I walked across the aisle to the row of telephones and dialed the therapy office where I'd been getting help.

"I need to get in tonight," I said. "Can I stop by on my way from the airport?"

By the time I got there, grayness and numbness had replaced the feeling that had surfaced at the airport. I could remember the rage, but I no longer felt it.

It was dark when I got home. The neighbors had cordoned off the street with sawhorses. Fifteen or twenty people bundled in winter attire gathered around a small bonfire in the street. The neighborhood Christmas caroling party. I parked the car a block away and sneaked in the back door of the house.

The house was dark and cold. Nichole was gone. I wandered into the living room. The fireplace was one reason I chose this house, I thought. And I don't know how to build a fire. Shane did that.

I sat down, looking at the half-decorated Christmas tree, the magic tree from last year. It didn't feel magical now. There were two gifts under it, small purchases I had made for Nichole. We had decided to avoid Christmas as much as possible this year.

I wondered where that part of me had gone, the part that still believed in Santa, in magic. My mind floated to another Christmas, ten years earlier. We had been dirt-poor then, living in the old yellow house on Pleasant Avenue. The children were young, Nichole maybe only six. I bought a scraggly tree that year. We had no decorations, so the children and I decided to make some. We took watercolors, painted what were supposed to be tin soldiers and reindeer faces on clothespins, then stuck them on the tree. A few neighborhood children came over. We strung popcorn and cranberries. We didn't have much, but there was magic in the air that year.

"Listen," I said to the children. "Be very still. I think I can hear it."

Their eyes got wide.

"Sleigh bells," I said. "Can you hear them?"

Megan smiled at me. Beamed. She had straight hair cut in a bob and a face full of freckles. "I think I can," she said.

Maybe she did. Maybe we all did. But seven years later, at age fifteen, she committed suicide.

How in God's name can this life and this world be like this? I thought. How can life be so magical and breathtakingly pure one moment, and so tragically, unbearably, heartbreakingly, stinking cruel and hurtful the next? People say this is good?

I looked at the three stockings hanging on the mantle, turned off the light, and left the room.

When Nichole arrived home a short time later, I was sitting at the kitchen counter. I looked at her. She looked at me.

"Merry Christmas," I said.

"Yeah, right," she said.

I stood up and grabbed my coat. "Come on. We've got to get out of here."

I drove to a nearby shopping mall. We walked around, looked at the window displays, then stopped to sit for a while by the huge mall Christmas tree, near the bottom of the escalator. Nichole nudged me.

"Look, Mom," she said, pointing to the top of the escalator. "Here comes Echo!"

The escalator moved her slowly toward me. Her head was turned. She was looking in another direction, toward the opposite side of the mall. How long had it been now since we talked? Six months? What had we argued about? I couldn't remember. She stepped onto the landing and began walking away.

"Go after her," Nichole said.

I sat there.

"Go talk to her, Mom. This is stupid."

I shook my head. "I can't," I said.

Nichole started chattering at me, scolding me. Music blared through the loudspeakers. I could hear the buzzing of voices around me.

"Melody. You're Melody, aren't you?"

The woman's face looked vaguely familiar. I should know her, I thought. But I can't remember.

She told me her name. "My husband used to work with your ex-husband," she said. Then she asked how I was.

"Well," I said, "pretty good. It's hard. . . ."

We made small talk, then I was finished. "Good to see you again," I said.

I turned to Nichole. "Let's go see Santa."

I started to stand up, then realized the woman was still staring at me, looking at me in the oddest way. It took me a moment to shake loose of her gaze. I stood up.

Nichole and I hurried away.

We sat on Santa's lap. "So," he said, "what do you two want for Christmas this year?" A light flashed. We got down, stood in line, and waited for our picture.

Nichole looked at it and shook her head. "Are you supposed to be crying on Santa's lap?" she asked.

"Sometimes, baby," I said. "Sometimes."

There was only one thing I wanted for Christmas. Only one thing I wanted in my life. I couldn't have that, now or ever. And if I couldn't have what I wanted, I didn't want anything at all. Just let go, I used to tell myself. Just let go. Well, this time I couldn't. Didn't want to. And maybe sometimes part of letting go is hanging on.

The holidays passed. Time always passes. But over the following weeks, whatever invisible force had allowed me to get up and at least give the appearance of being functional left. I started taking to my bed and staying there. I couldn't get up, couldn't move around.

I couldn't fight it anymore. I stopped getting massages. I couldn't stand to be touched. I stopped doing crossword puzzles.

I had made an effort, throughout this entire ordeal, to stay in the moment, stay with my feelings, feel whatever I needed. Although I was surrounded with fog and doubt, some part of me had still believed that if I stayed with this thing, if I kept swimming across this sea, it would lead somewhere. I'd find land. Now that belief left, too. There was no guidance. No getting through this. No getting around this. No getting out.

The part of me that squared my shoulders, bounced back, got up, and kept going no matter what had disappeared. My warrior spirit was gone, and I didn't know how to get it back.

I began to have dreams, wakeful visions. In them I could see my tombstone.

"Mom, get up," Nichole said, tapping on my bedroom door one evening. "Michael's here to see you."

I dragged myself out of bed. Michael, Echo's brother. How long had it been since I'd seen him? Seen anyone? I put on my robe and went downstairs. I offered him a beverage, poured myself a glass of water, and sat down. I asked how he was doing, how the children were.

He started to answer, then stopped. Through my fog, I could tell he was looking at me, looking at me the same as the woman at the mall.

"Geez, girl," he said. "You have no life force left in you. You've taken this right to the edge. Maybe you've taken it too far."

"What do you mean?"

"You're in trouble, girl," he said. "You look like you're almost gone. If you don't do something, I'm afraid you're going to die." He paused for a moment. "And soon."

His words stung, slapped me. I now understood the look, the one on his face, the one on the woman's face. They were staring at a dead person.

I talked some to Michael that evening, but it was hard to get words out. It was hard to believe any of this was happening. Hard to believe that in one year I had gone from the best year of my life to losing my son, my family, my work. And now I was losing me.

It wasn't that I wanted to die. I was torn. Excruciatingly, unbearably, viciously torn. I was treading water in the middle of a deep, dark river. I had one child standing on each side calling to me, and I didn't know which way to swim.

The next day I had to get out of bed. Ahmos, my manager, had flown into town. He was working at the office in my house, conducting a meeting with several other people. I sat in on some of the meetings, but I couldn't pay attention. Michael's words haunted me.

I can't die. I can't leave Nichole, I thought. I adore her. I can't do that to her now, on top of everything else. I felt terrified, paralyzed. I didn't know what to do. I had been doing everything I knew . . . .

The office door flew open, interrupting my private dialogue and the business meeting. Nichole flounced into the room. "What's everyone doing here?" she asked.

"What are you doing home from school?" I said. "It's the middle of the day."

"What are you doing out of bed?" she asked. "It's the middle of the day!"

"Leave," I ordered in my firmest parental voice.

"I'll leave, all right," she said. She walked out, slamming the door.

I excused myself and raced upstairs after her, following her into her bedroom. She plopped on the bed, picked up her telephone, and started to dial.

"Hang that up," I said.

She rolled her eyes.

"Don't you ever talk to me that way again," I said. "Not in public. And not when we're alone."

"Leave," she said. "This is my room."

I walked over to the bed. "I won't leave," I said. "We're going to discuss this."

The discussion didn't work. One thing led to another. I can't remember how it happened. The next thing I knew, I was sitting on top of her. She was half a foot taller than me, thirty pounds heavier, and there I was, sitting on top of her, pinning her down on her bed.

"This can't go on," I screamed. "You've got to start caring again. You've got to start caring about life again."

She looked at me.

"What about you?" she said.

Her words defused me. I stood up. Have I lost my mind? I wondered, walking downstairs. When I walked by the office, Ahmos asked if I was okay.

"Yes," I said.

"Mother-daughter stuff?" someone asked.

"Yeah," I said. "Mother-daughter stuff."

I went in my bedroom, closed the door, and sat on the edge of the bed. Nichole's words stuck in my mind. What about me? What about me caring about life again? How could I expect her to do something I couldn't do? What was I supposed to do? If you do everything you can, and nothing works, what's left? I was out of ideas.

The conversation had been an innocuous one. Now, it filtered slowly into my mind from nowhere. The gentleman had sat next to me on the plane, chatting politely during take-off. Told me about his business, his wife, his children. Said life was great. Had quite a scare last year though, he said. He'd gotten bored with life, with the grind. Started wondering if it was worth it. A month later, his gall bladder went bad, and he had to have it removed. Then he developed peritonitis. Before he knew it, a priest was standing by his bed administering last rites. As he heard the closing prayer, a thought penetrated his consciousness and he made a decision. He didn't want to die, not yet. He wanted to live. Within hours, his illness reversed.

My mind strained to recall his words. Something about the will to live. The will to live, he had said, can sometimes be stronger than anything else. Sometimes it can override whatever else is going on.

After Ahmos and the others left, I went into my office and turned on the computer. I couldn't do much about my pain. I was stuck with it, at least for a while. Maybe forever. I didn't know what the truth was about lessons, about this life, about the next. But I knew one thing. I didn't want to leave this way. Through the murk and fog in my mind, I wrote two letters. The first was an agreement.

"God, I'm still mad, not pleased at all. But with this letter, I commit unconditionally to life, to being here and being alive as long as I'm here, whether that's another ten days or another thirty years. Regardless of any other human being and their presence in my life, and regardless of events that may come to pass. This commitment is between me, life, and you. And although I'm not sure now if I want to live, I'm willing to want to. Help me come alive again. Please."

I printed the agreement, signed and dated it, then stuck it in my metal safe-deposit box.

The second letter was an afterthought. It came with startling intensity from the depths of my being.

"I don't know who you are," I wrote, "where you are, or if you even exist. I've thought about you a lot over the years, wondered what you look like, what your name is. I used to search for you, search crowds for your face, wondering, is he here? Is my soul mate in this room? This city? It's not that I'm impatient. I've been alone a lot of years. But it's time. I need your help, I need you. If you're out there, please come now."

I turned off the computer, went down to the living room, and studied the fireplace.

Maybe I could learn to build my own fires.

# Eight

....................

One cannot base one's conduct on the idea that everything is determined. . . . Instead, one has to adopt the effective theory that one has free will and that one is responsible for one's actions. Is everything determined? The answer is yes, it is. But it might as well not be, because we can never know what is determined.

—STEPHEN W. HAWKING, *BLACK HOLES AND BABY UNIVERSES AND OTHER ESSAYS*

I DEPLANE AT THE SANTA ANA AIRPORT AND hail a cab. I've rented a studio in Laguna for a few weeks and set up shop there. I need an infusion of sun, ocean, and fresh air while I finish this book. A two-day round trip to Minneapolis to connect with Nichole, then on to Milwaukee for a speaking engagement. Twenty below in both cities.

Now, the only thing that sounds good is watching a movie on TV.

I arrive at the apartment in Laguna, turn on the lights, and smile. A yellow note is taped on the computer: To turn computer on, unplug TV and plug in. A note on the answering machine: To hear message, press bar. I press it. "Hope your trip went well. Welcome back. Love you." I sit down on the bed. A VCR is hooked up. *Out of Africa* is partially inserted with another note taped to the television: To watch movie. . . Well, do I love you? Yes. . . turn TV on and push in.

He says the reason I like *Out of Africa* is because the love story is bittersweet. These are my favorite lines: "He began our friendship with a gift. And later . . . he gave me another. An incredible gift. A glimpse of the world through God's eye."

. . . . . . .

It happened fast, the way grass suddenly shoots up and covers the yard with green. I know I got carried away, but I didn't mind. It had been a long time since anything had carried me off.

He called himself a knight. Said his armor was rusty, but he was still a knight. And a wizard, like in days long ago. But when I asked him to teach me about magic, he said he couldn't.

"I'll show you," he said. "But you must remember what you already know."

But I'm getting ahead of my story.

Winter dragged on that year, turning almost imperceptibly into spring. Committing to life hadn't changed my life much that I could see. I felt a little more resolved, though, like someone getting ready to tackle an unpleasant chore.

One day at a cafe, I overheard a woman sitting at a table next to me. "My life is gray," she said. "It's not that I want a crisis or anything like that. I'm beyond that. But my life has no color."

I knew what she meant. I hated the grayness of my life, the lack of passion for anything.

Instead of sloshing through the first anniversary of Shane's death, Nichole and I decided to return to the house in the Virgin Islands where the three of us had stayed a year and a half ago, our castle by the sea. I invited my brother and sister and their families to come.

When we stepped through the door, I knew we had made a mistake returning to that house. Any comfort I had hoped to find from cherished memories wasn't there. It only reminded me of what had been lost. I looked at Nichole. I could tell she felt the same way.

We tried to be brave, but it didn't work. She snapped at me each time I looked at her. I burst into tears each time we sat down for a meal. Family members insisted it was okay for me to cry, but it didn't feel okay. I was tired of it. You can't go back, I thought. Can't go back in time, recreate the past. I wasn't yet able to pull the past to me, to cherish memories. Memories weren't a comfort yet; they still made me cry.

The Friday after we returned home, Nichole came home late. When I tried talking to her about it, she started giggling, then blew me a kiss.

She reeked of alcohol.

The next day we had a talk. I set some ground rules, trying to be clear and reasonable, understanding she probably didn't have much more to give than I did. I insisted that she begin seeing a counselor more frequently. She had gone for therapy off and on since Shane's death, but lately, she had stopped altogether, saying she didn't want to, didn't need to. I asked her how much she'd been drinking. She named only two other occasions in the past year, the day after the funeral and once last summer. She assured me she was doing all right, said she'd start going to counseling weekly.

I was torn between compassion for anything she might try to do to cope with her pain and feeling I should do something as her mother, as a responsible parent. I didn't know what to do. I didn't know how to help my daughter or even if I could. Despite my new resolve, I still wasn't sure what to do to help myself.

By the time the last patches of snow melted, I began to feel a clearer sense of change in me. A new determination arose to lighten some of the darkness that clung to me and at times still engulfed me. I had become bitter and resentful without realizing it. In the recesses of my mind, almost hidden from consciousness, was a list of reasons to be angry at almost everyone, including myself. I began deliberately working at forgiving people, trying to forgive myself.

I felt terribly ashamed since Shane's death. I didn't understand why. I just did. I felt hopeless, forgotten by God.

Maybe the dark cloak of grief was a necessary garment, worn to hide and protect me while I healed. But now it was time to shed it.

I still couldn't work. Whenever I sat at my desk I felt overwhelmed and instantly tired, so weary I had to lie down and sleep. My hands and arms ached too much to hold them in position to type. I started doing crossword puzzles again, planted an herb garden, became more health conscious. For two weeks I fasted on vegetable and fruit juice, hoping to help clear myself out.

And then I knew, the way people know things, that Echo and I would soon come back into each other's lives.

The reunion was sweet. Echo and I hugged and visited, and soon it felt like we had never been apart. We promised never to argue like that again.

"I missed you," she said. "I really worried about you this winter."

"I missed you, too," I said.

"I suppose you haven't heard," she said. "Scotty's back in town."

How long had it been. Twenty years?

The barbecues were Echo's idea. She likes social gatherings, entertaining and cooking. "Let's get together on Sunday. I'll cook," she promised. "We can all hang out. Just like the old days."

I was genuinely glad to see Scotty, but I didn't let myself know it, not right away. The three of us decided to get together every Sunday and try to round up some other people from our old crowd.

We had been a Get Along Gang back then. Being together now felt safe, felt good. I was shy and reserved around Scotty, like I had been twenty years ago. We had almost dated back then. We'd flirted and skirted around each other, the way people do when they're attracted to each other. But I had my sights set on someone else. No matter what, I was determined to marry this other guy. And I did. Started having babies. Next thing I knew, Scotty was gone, and the rest of our gang spread out over different parts of the country.

I had stayed close to Echo, though, and she had kept tabs on Scotty over the years. He'd gotten married, divorced, had his share of troubles. Had a child.

It happened fast. The first time he touched me was at the first barbecue. He asked how I was doing. I said not good, my heart was broken. He was chopping tomatoes and lettuce for the salad when I said it. He put down the knife, wiped his hands, walked up to me, and stood close.

By then, tears were running down my face.

I tried to brush them away, started to turn away. He put his hands out and gently cupped my face. I know, he said, I heard. I've got a child. I can't imagine. I'm sorry, he said.

We were talking one night, talking about how he ended up back in Minneapolis after all these years. I said it was for health reasons. He said that was true, but there was more to it than that.

"What?" I asked.

He looked at me. "Don't you know?" he said. "I came back to get you."

He told me things. Said he loved me, had since first he'd laid eyes on me twenty years ago. Said he'd always remember walking over to the table at the cafeteria one day, the first day we spoke, when we were each sitting with friends.

"Took me five minutes to get up the courage to stand up. Each step felt like a mile. And I was just walking over to say hi."

Said he had told his best friend way back then how he felt. Didn't know what he could do about it though, he said. You were determined to run off with someone else.

He told me something else one night. It

was dark in the house, except for a small light in the living room. He looked at me and said, "You've got to get up. You've got to get up." He said it loud and hard. "What do you have to do before you can do anything else? You've got to get up!"

"I am up," I said quietly.

"No," he said, "you're not. You're pumping air. Breathing. Walking. You've got to get up."

"I can't," I said.

"Yes, you can," he said back.

He didn't have to tell me his story. I already knew. Twenty-five years earlier, when he was seventeen, he had enlisted in the Marines, a warrior eager to serve his country, eager to run off to battle. In training camp one day he crumpled to the ground. Couldn't get up. Later he was diagnosed with Guillain-Barré syndrome, a neuromuscular disorder. For months he was paralyzed from the neck down. Over time, some of the paralysis subsided, but life never did return to the muscles in his legs. He had learned to live with, work around this so well that when I first met him, I didn't know. I thought he sauntered.

Only later did I realize his legs barely worked.

He held me. My tears scorched his face and chest.

The ring was Scotty's idea. He called one day and said, "I want to get you a ring. A Shakespearian poesy ring. A symbol of our love."

"I don't believe in love anymore," I said.

"Let's make some dreams," he said.

"It's too late," I said. "They're all gone. I can never have them, not what I want. It's too late."

"Make some new ones," he said.

"All I have is memories," I said.

"Let's make some new memories. Marry me," he said.

"It'll never work," I said.

"Then divorce me," he said.

And he told me one more thing: Come to consciousness.

# Nine

"It's nothing personal," he said. "It's just how the universe works."

SHE'S TRIED TO TELL ME THIS STORY BEFORE. Now I'm ready to listen. I pick up the phone and dial her number. "Tell me what it was like, Mama," I say. "Tell me about the time you almost died."

"It was forty years ago. I was on the operating table, under anesthetic. They were removing a tumor. I never did well with anesthetic.

"Suddenly I was on top of the room looking down at myself. I saw a world I'd never seen before. It was beautiful, so pretty. The colors, the shapes, the sounds. Oh, it resembled this world. I could see that everything was what it was. I could tell a tree was a tree, a bird was a bird. Only the edges weren't so clear. Everything was really part of the same thing. It was all one."

"Why did you come back?" I ask quietly.

"I don't know. But I knew this: I wasn't done yet. I had to come back to my body, to my life, to this world."

. . . . . . .

We danced that summer. We danced to the music of the universe. One day he took me

139

to a bookstore. I asked him what we were going to buy.

"Nothing," he said. "You're going to listen."

We sat on a ledge and he began reading from Kahlil Gibran. "For life goes not backward nor tarries with yesterday." He read to me a lot. No one had ever read to me before. He read me stories about Winnie the Pooh and all the creatures in the Hundred Acre Wood. He read to me from mysteries, the old ones. "Someone had murdered a Munchkin," began Kaminsky. He told me the story of Raymond Chandler's life, pumping out his classic tales until his beloved wife died and his writing ground to a stop.

History, he said. Remember history. Remember what you learned in science class. Remember the myths.

I said I wasn't good at history or science.

He said I could learn.

"The stories are ancient and timeless," he said. "As ancient and timeless as the struggles."

He told me about King Arthur and the knights of the Round Table. Archimedes, the wise old magical owl. Merlin, the magician. Avalon. And Camelot.

He told me to read Stephen Hawking's *A Brief History of Time.* Hawking, called by some the most brilliant theoretical physicist since Einstein, had translated his brilliance into a layperson's guide to understanding the complex nature of time and the universe, how and why things work in our world.

I struggled through the pages, reading and rereading paragraphs and chapters, trying to focus, trying to understand.

"What did you learn?" he asked weeks later when I had finished.

"Left to themselves, things deteriorate," I said.

"What else?" he asked.

I took a deep breath. "That Hawking wrote the book after being diagnosed with ALS, Lou Gehrig's disease, and after a tracheostomy, which removed his ability to speak."

Scotty didn't say anything. He let me decide what I was learning. Later he read to me from the introduction to Hawking's book.

"Did you hear that?" he asked.

"Yes," I said. Hawking had called himself fortunate. Fortunate except for the misfortune of having that disease.

He read to me from the Bible.

He reminded me of the tale of Pandora's box.

"What was the one thing left in it after all the evils had been allowed to escape into the world?" he asked. "What's the one thing people must have to survive?"

"I can't remember," I said.

"Think," he said.

"Oh," I said. "Hope."

"There are only three things that are important: faith, hope, and love," he said later, much later, when things had changed again. "When I met you I was cynical, but I still believed in God. The one thing I didn't have was hope. You helped me find that again," he said. "And it really hurts me to see you without it."

Since Shane's death, I'd been walking around breathing air, but I wasn't fully here. I wasn't fully participating, wasn't really living. My heart and soul weren't present. Now I was doing more than coming back. I was learning a new way of being here.

He dragged me to museums and art galleries.

"Look," he said. "Look at that. And that. And that."

"I see," I grumbled.

"No, you don't. Learn to look differently. Learn to feel what you see."

Monet became my favorite. I didn't know at first what impressionism was, but I instantly knew I liked the gentle way he saw the world. The way the soft hues of purple, pink, and green meshed into each other with less clearly defined boundaries than in paintings by other artists.

"You just like him because you don't wear your glasses enough, and that's how the world looks to you," he said. "Blurry."

"No," I said. "I don't think that's it."

Now I know why I like Monet. Maybe in his old age, and even with cataracts, he saw the world more clearly, saw it as it really is. Like Mama said, everything's part of the same thing.

One late afternoon Scotty told me to grab my sweater, we were going to a show.

"Which one?" I asked.

"You'll see," he said.

He drove me to a quiet spot at Lake Calhoun and parked the car. We walked over and sat on the grass.

"Feel it," he said. "Feel the grass. The earth."

"I do," I said. "What about the show?"

"Watch."

The sun began to descend to the horizon. Rings surrounded the glowing ball. It hazed over, bubbled out, as it lowered before our eyes. As it dropped below the edge, streaks of pink and orange fanned out from each side, at first coloring the clouds, then changing their very shapes.

"That was nice," I said, getting up.

"Sit down," he said, grabbing my hand. "It's not over yet."

Slowly, over the next ten minutes, the sky changed shades. The air cooled. Even the water on the lake looked different.

"See how everything changes?" he asked. "Do you really see?"

He pointed out people—young people, old people. Listen to them talk, he'd say. Listen:

"Grandma got hit on the head with a coconut and went unconscious."

"No. Grandma was drunk and passed out."

"Grandma got hit on the head. . . ."

"Aren't they great?" he'd say.

One night he took me outside.

"See that?" he said.

"All I can see is fog," I said.

"Ah, have you forgotten Merlin already?" he asked. "That's not fog. It's dragon's breath. It's magical. When the dragon's breath comes, when the fog appears, it is a magical time, a mysterious time. Things begin to change."

And I wondered if that were true.

We watched shooting stars, looked at the moon, and watched the critters, as he called them. He could get them to eat out of his hand, the squirrels and the birds. He taught me to do it, too.

"They'll talk to you," he said. "And you can talk to them. But you've got to listen, listen with more than your ears, watch with more than your eyes."

We were tender and close and gentle and passionate. Sometimes we argued, argued and fought like I had never done before. I didn't want to at first. It didn't seem polite. The first time he got me to yelling, I didn't think I'd ever stop.

When I finished, he asked me how I felt.

Better, I said. And I did feel better, and a little stronger.

He said good, and we made up.

Sometimes we stayed up all night, just talking. Both of us would be surprised to see the sun coming up. We'd throw on our jackets, go outside, and watch the morning sunrise.

One day he pulled me into the living room. "See that?" he said, pointing to a pewter figurine by the fireplace. "There's a wizard in there. Can you see it?"

"There's a wizard in the chicken?" I said.

"It's a rooster," he said. "Look!"

I stared at it.

He pointed to the statue of a knight standing next to it. "The knight is empty," he said. "No life force. But look in the face of the rooster."

I stared harder. Then I could see it. I could feel it. The shriveled face of a wizard, buried inside the rooster.

"There is a life force in everything that is. Learn to see it, learn to feel it. Learn to feed the creatures and find the creatures and feel the life force."

He talked about trolls and leprechauns, and slowly I began to see them. Whales, dolphins, and gnomes, hidden in the branches of a tree, peering through the gnarly bark.

One day, I showed him. "See that?" I said.

"What?" he said.

"There's a dragon in those trees."

He stared. The greenery on top of the group of trees formed a perfect, fire-breathing dragon.

"What does it mean?" I asked.

"It means something good," he said gently. "You're beginning to recognize the life force in the world around you because you're beginning to see it in yourself."

We went to the mountains. We went to the beach. He told me about the desert. We remembered places we had been and places we hadn't. Sometimes we slipped into churches when nobody was there and knelt and prayed.

There is a place in Laguna where the desert meets the ocean. At night the sky is lit with stars, and a mesquite fire burns close by. All the elements are present. All the elements connect here. This is where we were the night I realized I was finding that connection in myself.

. . . . . . .

The end came fast, as fast as the beginning. It happened in the fall. It was hard and hurtful, as many endings are. We were unforgiving, both caught up in our own pain and fear.

"I can't do it," I said. "I can't do traditional, don't want to do traditional. It's too late. All those years I wanted it, it wouldn't come. Now it's here, and I don't want it anymore. Damn it, it's too late. I can't blend families. I've raised my children alone too long. Those were yesterday's dreams. I'm just not ready, and neither are you."

He had things to do; I had things to do. I needed to do them by myself.

The day I took him to the airport, I took off the ring he'd given me.

"Don't you want it anymore?" he said.

"No," I said.

"Then throw it away," he said.

I tossed it into the wastebasket, and he boarded his plane.

He called it the winds of change. I called it another loss.

When Nichole came home that evening, I was running around the house, swooping up everything Scotty had given me and throwing it away.

"What are you doing?" Nichole asked.

"Throwing away his gifts," I said.

And when I said it, the minute I said it, something came over me. And I remembered the time in my life when Shane was born. And his smile and his love and his presence helped me go on at a time when I didn't think I could keep going. And he taught me to laugh and to play. And I started writing. And I learned to love myself more. And I learned to love people more. I learned to love God more. Because of Shane, I learned to love life more.

So I dug all the presents Scotty had given me out of the trash.

Maybe it was time to stop throwing away gifts.

# Ten

"A good warrior learns to respect the seasons and cycles of life," he said. "They're part of nature; they're part of you."

THERE'S A KNOCK ON THE DOOR. I OPEN IT. It's Scotty. "Ready for a break?" he says. The guy who wrote an Eagles hit song is jamming at a place downtown.

I grab my jacket. It's a southern California winter, about sixty degrees. We walk the few blocks to downtown Laguna, listening to the surf pound. The sky is lit with stars. The moon is a three-quarter chunk of light.

We get there and listen to four men in their forties and fifties play yesterday's songs.

I like two songs best. "We'll Meet Again Someday."

And "Peaceful, Easy Feeling."

. . . . . . .

It was noon on Monday, two weeks after Scotty left. I remember the day clearly. I always will.

I puttered in the kitchen. I had finished the crossword puzzle and was looking for something else to do. Still wasn't working, couldn't work, didn't know where or how to begin. But I had disassembled the shrine in my office, the memorial to Shane.

I still felt hurt and angry about the way things had ended between Scotty and me. Didn't know where he was now or what he was doing. Didn't want to, I told myself. But in my storm I knew something that only two other people in the world—Nichole and Scotty—knew. Even if Scotty hadn't saved my life, which I believed he had, he had brought me back to it.

The kitchen door flew open.

Nichole stood there.

"What are you doing home from school?" I asked. "It's the middle—"

"I need to talk to you," she said. "I need to talk right now."

I could tell she meant business. "Let's go up to my office," I said.

We sat across from each other.

"What's going on, honey?" I said.

She just looked at me. "Give me a minute," she said. "This is hard."

The clock on the wall ticked.

"I don't know how to say this," she said. "So I'll get it out the best I can. I can't control when I drink, how much I drink, what I do when I drink. If I'm around people that use, I can't not use. I can't help myself. I don't just drink too much, sometimes I go blank. I don't know what I'm doing. And the next day, I can't remember anything. I'm scared. I need help."

"Okay," I said. I didn't know what else to say.

"I always said I wouldn't be like this, Mama. We talked about it. Talked about it a lot. I said I wouldn't do this. And I'm doing it. It happened to me. I hate it. I'm starting to hate myself. I've been lying to you, looking you right in the face and lying to you. A lot. About where I'm going, what I'm doing. I've used cocaine, marijuana, but I always go back to alcohol. Vodka. I like vodka.

"I scared myself. I used cocaine and it felt like I was gonna stop breathing and I got scared and said I'd never use it again. And then the next day I used it again.

"Help me," she said.

I took a deep breath. This is good, I thought. I tried to sound calm. I told her, "What you're doing right now is good. Excellent, in fact. Give me some time," I said. "I'll make some calls."

"No, Mama," she said. "If I walk out of this house, I'll use some more. Everyone I know uses. I can't stop myself. I want help now."

The next day I drove her to an in-patient chemical dependency treatment center for young people. We brought in her suitcases, did some paperwork, took a short tour. Then it was time for me to leave.

We hugged good-bye. She clung to me, tears running down her face. She was stunning, beautiful, almost six feet tall, so statuesque. But at this moment she looked like she did when she was three.

I held her close. "It'll be all right, baby," I said. "It'll be good here. I think you're going to love it. It's a new beginning, the start of the rest of your life."

"I've hurt you," she said. "I feel so bad. I want you to be proud of me some day, Mama," she said.

"I'm proud of you now, honey," I whispered. "I always have been."

It was a strange time when Nichole was in treatment. I wandered around that big house all alone, but didn't feel as lost as I had before.

About a week before Christmas I went

down to the storage room, dug out the tree, the magic tree, and lugged it upstairs. I spent a whole day putting it up, getting the branches positioned. I carefully unpacked the hearts, the birds, the beads, and found a place for each decoration on the tree.

I unpacked the train. Sat on the floor, put the track together, then turned on the switch. The train chugged and whistled its way around the track. The tree glowed in soft pink lights. And my angel sat on top. The stockings, three of them, hung on the fireplace. "Joy to the World" played softly in the background.

I was glad I had bought that tree two years ago. I'd always have it. And now I had something else, something I didn't think I'd ever find again. Calmness, a sense of peace. It surprised me. It came from nowhere.

Echo and I went Christmas shopping.

I felt happy but confused. Shopping, being around all these people, scared me. Deciding who to buy a gift for and what to buy felt overwhelming. How shattered have I been? I wondered.

"Don't panic," Echo said. "Just let it come

from your heart. You'll know what to do."

Echo was right. I'd find myself standing in a store, then I'd see something and know it was the right gift. Mickey Mouse for Nichole. She loved Mickey. And that little girl I had left at treatment surely needed a toy, something to hug and hold. A hat for Louie. He loved hats. By the end of the night, without a list, I had finished all my shopping. Went right to each gift.

And I began to wonder if that's how things were going to be from now on. I wouldn't have to panic anymore. All I needed to do was get quiet and listen, and I'd hear the answer in my heart. I'd be led right to what I was looking for, even if I didn't know what that was.

After we finished shopping we went to a restaurant. While we ate pancakes and drank coffee, we talked about separations and reunions. We decided that sometimes people come into your life, and when they leave you feel bad and miss them for a while, but you get over it.

But other times, people come into your life and you're so close and love each other so much that it matters a lot when they're gone. You have a big hole in your heart, an empty spot that doesn't go away. But you learn to live with, work around, this hole in your heart until you're reunited.

Other people might not understand this, we decided, but it didn't matter as long as Echo and I understood each other.

We decided something else, too. We decided that sooner or later you had to learn to live without almost everybody, at least for a while. Even people you didn't think you could live without.

But no matter how long it took, it looked to us like love always found itself again.

. . . . . . .

Christmas was a quiet day. I took Nichole's presents to her at the treatment center. They wouldn't let her come home. She fussed about that. We had always been together at Christmas, but we decided it was okay, that this was still a good Christmas. She opened her gifts, and we visited for a while in the cafeteria. Her dad visited her, too. That made her happy.

She was working hard on herself. She had decided that she liked treatment, liked learning what she was learning.

"I feel like a new person," she said. "Mama, I'm so happy I'm here."

I could see that. She glowed.

The following week was family week. It meant attending lectures and groups with other parents to learn more about our children, chemical dependency, and more about ourselves. I felt a little uncomfortable, but it didn't matter. I felt determined to do this for Nichole. For me. Wouldn't miss it for the world.

I kept fairly quiet that week, listening to lectures about the disease of alcoholism, getting tips on how to handle different situations after your child came home. The days passed quickly. But as the week wore on, we all dreaded the same event: family conference.

By now we all knew what family conference meant. This was the day the dirty laundry got hung out to air. The parents, the child, and the counselor would have a private session in the counselor's office. In that room, the child would talk and say everything he or she ever wanted or needed to say to that parent. Feelings about things the parent had or hadn't done, feelings the child needed to get off his or her chest, things the child had done that the parent didn't know about. The parent got to talk, too.

Nichole was edgy. I was, too. The day before the conference we argued in the cafeteria during our visiting time. We each walked out on a sour note.

The next day I steeled myself as I walked into the small office. I sat down across from Nichole. The counselor, a woman with short-cropped hair, sat to the side.

First it was my turn. I didn't have much to say. I said Nichole and I had talked a lot about feelings. That I'd had a lot of reactions to her behavior over the past two years. I'd been hurt, angry, frustrated, and upset at times. I also said that we loved each other a lot and living with her had been pretty good, everything considered. I said I knew she'd been in a lot of pain, and so had I. And that some of the things she'd done, even during the time she'd been really wild and out of control, had been good and loving.

I said I was proud of her for being here, proud of her courage, proud of how hard she'd worked. And that I loved her.

Then it was Nichole's turn.

I was ready. Don't be defensive, I told myself. No retorts. Let her say it. Let her get it off her chest. I know I haven't been the best mother in the world. I know I've done some things wrong. Every parent has. Just listen to her talk about them and don't say anything back. Respect her feelings, let her have them.

I listened. Tried really hard not to feel guilty, but I knew I was shriveling in the chair.

God, didn't she know that more than anything in the world, I had wanted to give her a traditional family? But she got cheated. And I knew it was hard.

Nichole gently explained some of her feelings and grievances. I listened. We got through that.

Then she told me I was defensive. And I told her she was defensive. The counselor said maybe we both were. I said I felt guilty. Nichole said so did she.

"First part's over," Nichole said. "Now I

have to tell you the wrong things I've done."

She went down her list. It didn't surprise me. She had already told me most of those things, but she had to go over it again.

Then that part was finished. I took a breath and sat back. Almost through it, I thought.

"Tell her," the counselor said, looking straight at Nichole.

Nichole just sat there.

"Go ahead," the counselor said.

Nichole sat up straight. She looked at me, looked at her counselor, looked at her list. Her chin started shaking and her hands trembled. Her voice was soft in the beginning.

"I'm sorry, Mama. I didn't mean to do it. I feel so guilty. I feel so bad. I tried to drink it away. I tried to drug it away. I've run from it and I've run from it."

Then she stood up in the middle of the room, and she was yelling at the top of her lungs.

"Dear God, dear God in heaven, Mama, I feel so guilty. You told me. You told me to be home by six that night. That's the last thing you said before we walked out that door. And if I would have listened, if I would have been a good girl, if I would have minded and come home when you said, Shane wouldn't be dead. He'd be alive right now and you'd have a son and I'd have a brother and we'd have a family. This whole stinking nightmare mess is all my fault and I feel so bad and guilty and I'm so, so sorry, Mama. I didn't mean to do it. I never meant to do it. I love my brother and I love you."

The next thing I knew I was holding her. We were on the couch and I was holding her, holding her head to my chest and stroking her hair.

And her body shook so hard I could barely hold her.

And the secret was out.

I told her, told her it was an accident, but she already knew that. Told her it was nobody's fault, but she already knew that, too. I told her not to feel guilty. We'd talked about guilt for two years, and she had said she didn't feel that way. I told her not to feel that way now, but my words sounded weak and hollow. She needed something more from me.

The counselor handed us each a tissue. We

talked a little longer. Then the conference was over.

I walked to the dining hall, poured myself a cup of coffee, and sat down at a table. There was something, something I had to say. I couldn't leave her, not like this. This was my baby. I didn't know what to do, but I had to do something.

I took a sip of coffee. Just trust, I thought. It'll come.

I dug around in my purse and found a pen and a piece of paper. I wrote a note, folded it up, and tucked it in my pocket.

Nichole came out a few minutes later to say good-bye. We didn't say much. We had orders not to discuss anything that was said in family conference, at least not tonight.

We hugged good-bye. I reached into my pocket, took out the note, and slipped it into her hand. I said I loved her, and I left.

When I got home the telephone rang.

"Thank you, Mama," she said. "Thank you so much. That note meant a lot, more than anything."

It was a simple note. It was the truth.

"Dear Nichole, I love you very much. I always have. I always will. And if you had called me that night to ask if you could ski later than six o'clock, I would have said yes, you could stay longer. You didn't do it, baby. And don't ever again think you did. Love, Mom."

Right then and there, I learned how important it is to let people off the hook. I learned how important it is to let myself off the hook, too.

Nichole came home in January. We had a party. It was a grand day. The girls from the Get Along Gang were there—Joey, Carmen, and Ingrid. We had balloons and fruit juice. We played music and laughed. Nichole tried to explain to her friends what treatment was like, what her life was going to be like.

"We each go through different things," she told me later. "We know the other person doesn't understand, because they haven't been through exactly that same thing. But we listen, and we tell each other we don't exactly understand. But we care. That's what makes us a Get Along Gang. We help each other get along."

.......

It happened quickly, almost in a moment. Nichole had been home about three weeks. She had been struggling, trying to catch up at school. She felt awkward, embarrassed, out of place. Said she hated school now.

I'd been stuck in the house for two days. The garage door had frozen shut, and I couldn't unstick it. I was sitting in that house feeling trapped when it came over me, suddenly, powerfully, clearly.

**I'm not finished yet.**

It was a simple knowing that rocked my soul. Made me feel strong, powerful, like I hadn't felt for a long time. I stood up and said it aloud.

"I'm not finished yet."

When Nichole came home that night, I told her.

"Pack your bags, honey. We're going back."

"Where?"

"Back to the Get Along Gang," I said. "Back to Joey, Ingrid, Carmen. Back to your school, your friends. I'm going back to work. We're going back to life."

"Do you mean it?" she asked, her face already glowing. "It's been too painful for you to be in Stillwater. Are you sure?"

"Yes," I said. "I'm ready."

"What about the house? You've tried to sell it a couple times. It hasn't sold. What are we going to do? It's so big."

"I'll tell you what we're going to do," I said. "We're going to hold each other's hands, we're going to walk out that front door, and we're not ever gonna look back. We've got a year and a half until you graduate and leave for college. And we're going to have the best year together a mother and daughter ever had."

There are seasons of the heart. There are seasons in our lives, just as there are seasons to all of nature. These seasons cannot be forced any more than one can force the coming of spring by going out and pulling at tender blades of grass to make them grow.

It took me a while to understand. My warrior spirit wasn't gone; neither was Nichole's. We were being trained in the ways of the heart.

# Part III

# Eleven

....................

It takes courage to love.

—ANONYMOUS

On MY WAY BACK TO MINNEAPOLIS, I FLY TO Las Vegas to meet Louie. We haven't spent time together for a while. Seeing each other will be good.

We eat Chinese food. He calls it the best in the world. We take in a show. The first part is a magic act. I like magic. I ask him what's next.

"It's the monkey," he says. "The one I've been telling you about for years."

I watch as the monkeys do their routine. At the end of the show, when the trainer gives the signal, the orangutan rolls his big eyes, smacks his lips, and says, "Maw-Maw."

"I'll be," I say.

"I like animals that talk and don't know what they're saying," he whispers.

Later, before I catch the red-eye flight to Minneapolis, Louie starts talking about how he thinks the world is heading toward a time of healing, a time when people learn joy.

Then he looks at me, right into my eyes. "I used to worry about you," he says. "I don't anymore. Your heart is completely open.

And you've learned how to own your power."

Afterward, a photographer snaps a picture of each of us holding an orangutan. Nichole says it's a Kodak moment.

. . . . . . .

It was a simple thought. **I want to get a bird.**

It began with a public television special on birds, birds as pets. Scotty showed me. "Look," he said.

Scotty had come back into my life after the move, actually, on moving day. I had found a place quickly, a small town house in Stillwater. The moving crew showed up that morning but seemed befuddled and distracted. I talked to the foreman for a few minutes and learned his twenty-eight-year-old brother had died the night before.

As we all wandered around trying to figure out what to do next, the phone rang. It was Scotty. We had talked on the phone a few times. Not talked, argued. Now he said he knew it was moving day, and figured I might need some help.

Two things surprised me about the move. Except for a few pieces of furniture, nothing fit anymore. Even the decorations were clunky and outdated.

And starting over was harder than either Nichole or I had anticipated. Each step was uphill and required a great deal of effort— concentrated, focused effort. Neither of us would make this new beginning by being coddled. Instead, it would happen by our learning how strong we were.

Nichole was trying to discipline herself to get to school on time, get her homework done, get her grades up. She had now become frantic about getting into college.

I was trying to get back to work. I did a few speaking engagements but didn't have much to say. People were kind. They listened. But I wondered what I was doing and why.

For both of us, the simplest acts required an inordinate amount of effort and triggered a volcano of feelings.

On the second anniversary of Shane's death, we had spoken together at a grief conference in Texas. This had been a cathartic, healing event for us. It symbolized a turning point. But in many ways, Nichole had much more to say and share than I did.

I was still crying in private every day. And I had a case of the terrors I couldn't shake, no matter how much therapy I did, no matter how much of anything I did. The simplest acts, such as going to the gas station, over-whelmed me. More complicated events, such as speaking or attending a business meeting, sent me into a panic. I had to write out each word I intended to say for my speeches.

It was hard to trust life. I kept waiting for the rug to be pulled out from under me again. Nothing felt safe or secure.

I was amazed at how much my mental focus and concentration had been dis-turbed. Yet I was determined to overcome this, a determination I hadn't experienced for a long time.

One day I parked my car in front of a store that sold religious items. When I went in, the clerk asked what I was looking for.

"I don't know," I told her. "But I think I will when I see it."

I settled on a rosary, a beautiful one with red beads, and a metal cross on a leather necklace. I didn't understand why I pur-chased the rosary. I'm not Catholic. But I was drawn to it. I learned the Hail Mary and began reciting it over and over, holding the rosary in my hand.

"Hail, Mary, full of grace. Blessed are you among women. And blessed is the fruit of your womb, Jesus. Holy Mary, Mother of God, pray for us now and at the hour of our death. Amen."

On two occasions I slipped into St. Michael's Catholic Church in Stillwater. Once for a Sunday service, once for a communion service. As I stood in line waiting for the wafer and the wine, I hoped I wouldn't get caught sneaking into a Catholic communion service when I wasn't Catholic. But I needed this connection with ritual and with God.

I began to remember and practice other values that had served me well in the past. Service. Gratitude. The simple act of taking responsibility for myself and my life, each day, no matter what blows I'd been dealt, no matter how unfair life seemed. I had believed in and practiced these values for years, but I had been unable to practice them in a meaningful way since Shane's death.

I began to use other tools, too. I had read

that merely observing something meant interacting with it and that the simple act of observation changed it. I began the quiet act of watching myself, staying with myself.

I began to see that my emotions, like the sea, became colored by whatever storm was brewing. When the gale passed, the sun returned. I learned to wait for each storm to pass and trust that it would.

Although I was still unable to write, I enrolled in several university extension classes. I took an art appreciation class called "The Power of Seeing." I signed up for a course studying the myths and facts of King Arthur and the knights of the Round Table and another studying the spirituality in mystery writing.

At the end of the mystery-writing class, the teacher asked us to write a paper explaining what we had discovered about the spirituality in mysteries. We were to read our papers in class.

When it was my turn, I looked at the teacher and the other students gathered around the table where we sat.

"I didn't write a paper," I said. "For some

reason, I can't write yet. And I need to explain something," I said. "That I am even here, that I care enough to get out of my house, make the half-hour drive, and work through my terror enough to walk into this building is, to my way of thinking, a miracle.

"I didn't know if I was going to do this assignment," I said. "I didn't know if I could, or would, even finish the required reading. But late last night, I decided to. I stayed up until two in the morning. And this is what I've figured out.

"I'm sure the war between good and evil is part of it. I'm sure the whodunits are important, too. But to me, the spirituality in mystery writing isn't either one of those things. It's staying with the mystery, sticking with each word, sentence, and chapter until the end. Until the mystery is solved."

The members of the class looked at me. A blond woman, probably in her forties, spoke up.

"Didn't I see you in the King Arthur class?"

"Yes," I said.

"You're looking for the Holy Grail, aren't you?" she said.

Despite the grueling effort it took to live life each day, a rhythm began to emerge, a new rhythm that was as steady as a heartbeat. It couldn't be forced. But if I relaxed, trusted, and listened, I could connect with it, this new rhythm of life.

"I miss who I used to be," I said to my therapist during one visit. "I miss the ability I used to have to just do things, to make up my mind to do something and then do it."

"You still have your strengths," she said. "They're still there for you. Maybe you're learning about a new kind of power."

I began to sense what she meant when I sat with a friend through the death of her father.

The message was on the answering machine one afternoon. A friend needed me. Her father was dying. He was a friend and work associate of mine from twenty years ago. It had happened quickly. He had two, maybe three weeks to live. She hadn't seen him in years. He had only recently come back into town and into her life. They had resolved their differences. Within days, his liver failed, his stomach swelled, and he was hospitalized.

"I want to sit with him through this," she said. "I want to be with him through this. He doesn't have anyone else. But I'm all alone. Everyone I know is scared, scared of death, scared of this whole thing."

I told her I'd sit with her. But I was apprehensive as I walked through the hospital corridors to find her father's room. So many things triggered the horror of what I'd been through, brought it back as though it were yesterday. Being in a hospital was one of those things. When I entered the room and touched my friend's arm, I was surprised. I felt peaceful and strong. I clutched my rosary in one hand, the metal cross in the other. I asked her father if he would like the cross. He said yes. His daughter slipped it around his neck. We sat together, those weeks. I went as often as I could.

We talked, sat quietly, did all the things people do when they're waiting for someone to die. By now, her father was almost unconscious, barely aware of his surroundings.

One morning she called. "Come now," she said. "I know today is the day."

When I got to the hospital, she was upset.

"Something's wrong," she said. "I know he's ready to die. But there's a piece missing. I don't know what it is. Until we figure it out, he can't leave. And he's not coherent enough to tell us."

I took a deep breath. "It'll come," I said. "All we have to do is relax and listen."

We went downstairs to the soft drink machine in the lobby. While we were standing there sipping our sodas, a friend of her father's from years ago entered the hospital. He saw us and walked over to where we were standing.

"You haven't seen your dad much over the years, have you?" he asked.

"No," she said. "He just came back into my life. And now he's leaving."

"Did you know he was raised Catholic?" he asked.

"No, I thought he was Protestant," she said.

We both said it at the same time: last rites.

We called in a priest. Her father relaxed visibly. His breathing changed, vital signs changed. Hospital staff moved him to a private room.

"I'll leave you two alone," I said.

I went down to the coffee shop, ate a sandwich, and bought one for my friend. When I returned to the room, she was sitting in the chair. She looked tired, drawn. I offered her the sandwich.

She looked at her dad.

"Let's go outside," she said. "I need a break. I'll eat out there."

We sat at a small picnic area on the hospital grounds. She finished her sandwich and crumpled the wrapper. We looked at each other. The sun was shining brightly, warmly. About four birds had landed at our feet. They were sitting there chirping. A squirrel ran up to her feet and stood there on his hind legs, his little paws in a begging position.

I pointed to the creatures. "Aren't they great?" I said.

We walked back into the hospital. A nurse met us at the door. "I'm sorry," she said. "He just died."

I held her hand and said how sorry I was. I knew she had begun this journey, too, the journey to the heart.

A new rhythm now emerged in my relationship with Scotty. Although we lived fifteen hundred miles apart, he began to show up whenever I needed him or wanted to see him.

It was on one of these visits that I learned about birds. Scotty was flicking the remote control, changing the television from station to station, when he stopped at the special about birds.

The little bird they featured was scraggly and had lost most of his feathers. But he hopped around the house, rolled over on his back, and let his owner scratch his tummy. I was taken by his sweet, intelligent personality.

That's when I got the idea. I knew it was right. I turned to Scotty. "I want a bird."

We went to the pet store the next day. I looked at the parrots. I liked them, but I wasn't sure.

"If you're going to get a parrot," he told me, "get an African Gray."

He went on to praise this breed of parrot. As intelligent, some said, as monkeys. Vocabularies of hundreds of words, hundreds of sounds. Bonded with their owners. Lived to be seventy.

"Look at this," he said, pointing to an article in a bird magazine in the store.

The article detailed how one African Gray, when left at the veterinarian's, turned to the owner and said, "Please don't leave me."

That's when I knew I wanted a bird. And I wanted an African Gray.

"Okay," I said. "Where do I get one?"

I learned that would be complicated, too. The breed was difficult to find. Not a lot of them around, and you had to find the right bird for you, had to match personalities. We called around. Couldn't find any in the state. I didn't know what to do next.

But I wasn't worried. I knew I'd get my bird.

I was right. Louie found her in California and sent her to me for my birthday. I picked her up at the airport. Her name was Max.

I peered into the traveling cage. She was gray, about the size of a pigeon, and had red tail feathers. She looked at me.

"Well?" she said.

Max got sick soon after arriving in Minnesota. I was afraid she was going to die and I'd lose her, too. She had brought so much joy and lightness into our lives. We had bonded from the start. She had already begun imitating my laugh. I was surprised at how much she was laughing. I was surprised at how much all of us were laughing.

When I took her to the veterinarian, the doctor assured me Max would be fine. She asked me a few questions about how I handled the bird, how I interacted with the bird. "Carefully," I said. I didn't pick her up a lot. If I did, I wore oven mitts. When she got out of her cage, it sometimes took me hours to get her back in.

"It's not the bird I'm worried about," the doctor said. "It's you. That bird is dominating you. She knows you're scared of her. You've got to take charge with that bird."

I took a deep breath. "I'm not a bird expert," I said. "But from what I've read, this bird has three hundred pounds of pressure in her beak. Is that right?"

The doctor said yes.

"So in one swoop, she could take my finger off. Is that right?"

The doctor said yes.

"And you want me to stand up to her?"

The doctor said yes.

I took the bird home, put on my oven mitts, picked her up, and put her back in her cage. Then I went to my bedroom and watched two videos, videos I had watched many times over the past two years.

The first showed the basketball game, the one I had attended with Shane the morning of his accident. One of the mothers had been filming her son. She had been kind enough to make a copy of the tape and send it to me.

The second was a video of Shane's funeral. In my distress, I had asked someone to film it. I knew it would be the last memory I had of him. I knew I was too overwhelmed to remember much of what happened.

I watched the basketball game. Shane looked so vital, so full of life. I could hear his voice, yelling out to other team members. Then I watched the funeral clips, ending with hundreds of balloons soaring up into the sky, one trailing behind.

No wonder I've been so stunned, I thought. We went from basketball to funeral in a matter of days. As I sat there thinking all this, I sensed God watching me. For the first time in years, I sensed that this presence was watching me with love.

And then I wondered if life wasn't like the bird. You might know full well what it can do to you, should it turn on you. But sometimes you've got to square your shoulders, act like you're confident, get in its face, and stand up to it anyway.

I walked over to Max's cage. Stuck out my hand. She climbed on and looked at me.

"Hello," she said.

# Twelve

"Why should people bother to love if all they're going to get is a broken heart?" she asked.

"Because," I said, "love is what we do best."

I WALK THROUGH THE RESTAURANT ON MY way out the door. In the front lobby by the cashier, a picture hangs on the wall.

I've seen them before in shopping mall displays. The picture you see first is a plain repetitive print, somewhat like fabric. It doesn't make much sense artistically, but it's pleasant to look at.

Hidden within the design is another picture, a hidden picture, the real picture. One you can see only by looking in a certain way. The best way to develop this deeper vision, I've been told, is to relax, stop staring so hard at the details of the pattern, and look for the reflection of something else in the picture. While you focus on that reflection, they say, the real picture will emerge.

I've never had much luck with deeper vision and I've stared until I was cross-eyed. Today, I'm determined to conquer the picture.

I pay the cashier, pull up a chair, and sit down in the lobby. I'm not leaving until I see it.

I was on my way back to my hotel in Dallas when it hit me, hit me right in my heart.

**It's time for your message to change.**

I had just finished a one-hour speaking engagement. Speaking was hard. Even the limited amount of work I was doing strained me. But Ahmos thought it was time for me to begin accepting a few speaking engagements.

I wasn't as certain.

I didn't have much to say.

I had spent the last hour clutching my notes, reading each word verbatim from a prepared speech just in case the amnesialike blankness that had accompanied my grief struck while I was onstage. My story was honest and simple. But even I was tiring of it.

"My son died. I've been in pain. Struggling. Trying. But I'm still confused. It's still hard. Thank you very much. . . ."

I reminded myself all I had to do was speak from my heart, even if my message was confusion and hopelessness. But the real truth was, I didn't get it. I didn't get what this journey, this excursion, this experience, had been about.

My therapist kept saying I was trying to make sense of something that didn't make sense, might never make sense. Maybe I was. But I needed to find some meaning in all this.

I didn't get what my life was about. I was beginning to wonder if I ever would.

That's when I heard it again. **It's time for your message to change.**

I knew that was probably true. I had no idea what it meant, though. I shrugged it off, unlocked the door to my hotel room, and began packing and crying. That didn't surprise me. Crying had become a way of life since my son's death, something I did when I needed to do it. I laughed a lot, but I still cried when I needed to. And I needed to often.

Since I had begun my efforts to start over, to come back to life, I noticed a pattern. Whenever I took a step forward, experienced even a small success, I cried. It hurt to go forward without Shane.

It made me furious that I had to.

I stopped packing and did something I

hadn't done for a while. I started talking out loud to God.

"Okay," I said. "I'll do it. I will accept the fact that my son is dead. He's gone. For the rest of my life, he's gone and I can't do anything about it. But I don't care what people say about heaven and the afterlife and how happy he is now, I know Shane. I know how the three of us were together. I know how much we loved each other. And I *know* that wherever he is, he misses me. He misses us as much as we miss him. So I'll accept this, this whole nasty mess, and go on with my life. But I need you to do something for me. I need you to give him something. A gift. Something he can keep with him all the time. Something to remind him of how much we love him. Something he can keep nearby that will help him feel my love for him until we can be together again."

The room got still. I swear I heard this. Not with my ears, but in my heart, as clear as if I had heard it with my ears.

**And what would this be, this gift?**

I started pacing and thinking. I knew Shane. Better than anyone in the world, I knew my son. I knew what made him happy. I knew things he wanted, things he talked about, things he liked. Suddenly I knew the gift I wanted to send him. The only thing that would do.

A parrot that talked.

And at that moment I understood who had sent Max to me.

Max was Shane's gift to me to help my heart heal.

I cried and I laughed. My heart felt lighter already. And I started to release my balloon, the one I had been holding since the day of his funeral.

There were two things I wanted and needed. One I hadn't discussed with anyone. That was to make some sort of connection with Shane, even though he was gone. That had just happened.

The other was to heal my connection with God.

It was a strange night, that night when I got home. I had felt happier for a few hours after my realization about Max, but gradually I began falling into a pool. The angst, the blackness that rivets and smothers the soul, began to reappear. I was bringing to the surface my cold war with God.

It was fury and gall—not just about my son's death, although that was predominant and outstanding on the list. It was fury and gall about my life.

Since the day my soul and body hit this planet, life had not been what I expected.

A childhood that had gone on endlessly in the midst of a family in turmoil and pain. Beginning at age eleven to cross off the days until I would turn eighteen.

Stumbling around in the dark, groping my way toward maturity.

A marriage that I thought would be the marriage of my dreams, one that ended in divorce ten years later.

Years of struggling to overcome poverty and the aloneness, the overwhelming difficulty of being a low-income single parent.

Three years at the top of the mountain. Three years. Three of the best years of my life. Finally having a family and a life that worked. Dreams that came true.

Then falling down the other side of the mountain, losing it, spending the last years in deep emotional, psychic, mental, and sometimes physical pain, more pain than I thought any human being could or should have to live with and through. Having to face the choice of living without what I wanted most, or not living at all.

It didn't take a mathematical genius to add up these figures. Forty-two years of hard and painful struggle. Three years of joy, goodness, fulfillment.

Forty-two years of waiting for three.

Forty-two years of chasing dreams that didn't pan out.

I didn't get it. Not at all. I had spent years learning to look at the bright side, look at the positive, look at what's right. I'd spent years convincing myself I wasn't a victim. I was tired of the enormous amount of energy it took to continually keep convincing myself that this was good and right.

It didn't feel right. Or good.

For the most part, life had been a series of disappointments. And the scale escalated as time went on. I could have what I wanted, but there would be a catch. Always. I was tired of the hooks, tired of the tricks, tired of watching life slip through my fingers as soon as I grabbed it.

My life was one of three things: accidental, incidental, or deliberate. It didn't matter which one—each idea enraged me. If it was my fault, then why hadn't someone told me what I was doing wrong before I did it? What about the years when I had tried hard to do my best? My best sure hadn't changed things much either.

The cold war turned white hot. I was in the ring with God. I wanted an explanation. There didn't seem to be one. And, I wondered, how can you win a war with God?

I struggled and wailed in the depths of my soul until the wee hours of the morning. Whatever had sprung loose would not be stopped, tucked away, or eased.

Then in the middle of the night it happened. I knew what happened because it had happened twice before.

The first time, I was younger, about twenty-six, out of work with no prospects. I had already answered every ad in the paper, ruling nothing out. I was out of money, soon to be out of a home, and out of ideas. I was standing on the corner waiting for the bus when the angel spoke to me.

"Turn around," she said.

I did. I was standing in front of a bank. To the left was a doorway leading to a law firm on the second floor. "Go in and tell the man who runs the firm you're looking for a job. Tell him you want to work for him."

This is crazy, I thought. But the voice was so certain, so clear, so peaceful, I knew it could be trusted. I marched up the stairs and asked to talk to the attorney in charge. I walked in, stood in front of his desk, and told him I wanted a job, wanted to work for him.

"What a coincidence," he said after hearing me out. "I've been thinking I need to add another employee, but I haven't got around to advertising yet. Fill out an application."

Two weeks later, I started the job.

The second time, only eight years ago, I was again out of money and food. The children and I were hungry, down to one potato and a can of green beans. No money due to come in for over a week. I had tried to hold my head up and not ask for help. But I needed help now.

I drove to the local food bank. I walked up to the door. The sign said "Will Return Wednesday." It was Monday. I got back in the car, laid my head on the steering wheel, and cried. I was tired. Tired of the money struggles. Tired of the poverty. Tired of trying. Tired of trying to make ends meet that never met, no matter how hard I stretched them.

Then I heard the voice again, a soft whisper but sure and calm, telling me that soon I wouldn't have to worry so about money. Unless I wanted to.

Instantly I felt comforted, peaceful. I drove home, and we split the beans and potato among us.

There was no pot of gold on my doorstep, no winning sweepstakes entry in the mail. But a year later, the book I was struggling to write at the time hit the *New York Times* best-seller list.

Things got better—not because I had money, but because there was peace in my soul.

Now, in the midst of my angst, I heard the whisper again. The voice was calm and sure.

After tomorrow, you'll never see your life the same again.

I turned off the light and fell into sleep.

The next morning, my despair began anew, the turmoil picking up where it left off. I was frozen in my bed, flattened by my anguish.

Then the answer came gently, softly, and as certain as the morning sun, filling me with light.

Every experience I have had in my life has been about the same thing.

Each lesson has ultimately and absolutely been about one thing, the only thing that is.

Love.

I had heard it said before. Now I understood.

The struggles to learn I had a soul. My struggles to learn about my strengths. Even my grief. I had been talking to a woman seated near me at dinner one night, wailing about my pain, my anguish over losing my son, about how close the three of us had been, about the hole in my heart. The woman had turned to her husband. Have you ever loved that deeply? she had asked. I don't think so, he had said. Even these, my blackest and darkest moments, had been a form of love, one of its lessons. A harder one, but still a lesson of love.

I laughed out loud, alone in my room. What did I think love would look like? Feel like? Be? A romantic vision of being carried off to Camelot? And then what?

Forgiveness. Compassion. Service. Self-love. Loving myself when I was certain nobody else loved me or ever would. Then opening up, learning to let others in.

Faith.

Acceptance. Acceptance of myself, my life, others, their lives.

Friendship. Courage. Perseverance.

Hope.

Joy. Learning to deliberately choose joy. The simple sweet process of learning to be present each moment and find and choose joy, a joy not dependent on outer circumstances, but one that comes from the heart.

How did I think I would learn all these lessons, all these subcategories of love?

Trust. Trusting myself. Learning to trust others, life, God.

Learning to play and laugh. Learning to walk away, sometimes learning to stay put. Honoring my own needs, even when they differed from what others thought my needs should be. Honoring me, even when I was different from what others thought I should be. Trusting my vision for my life, creating another vision if that one didn't work. Chasing my dreams, catching them, then finding more. Learning about this connection, this absolute and divine connection to all that is, and maybe ever was, in the universe.

And finally, facing and accepting death.

Had I thought all those lessons would be learned easily?

I guess I had.

I saw now that even the struggles, the hard times when I cursed and moaned and whined, had not been punishment. God hadn't been peering down from the heavens saying, Good, let her crawl over broken glass for a bit. That will teach her.

God was saying, Look, she's learning to love.

The struggle of climbing to the top of the

mountain was as much my purpose as getting to the top of it.

I felt a lightness that I hadn't felt in years, maybe ever. For a moment I imagined I heard the angels sing, a celestial chorus of joy. I wondered how long, how long really, I had struggled to get this lesson right.

I didn't have to scramble up and down the ladder from despair to euphoria anymore, trying to convince myself that life was either painful and terrible or joyous and wonderful.

The simple truth was that life was both.

I hadn't come here to live happily ever after, although I now sensed I could. I had come here to learn love. That's what the lessons had been about.

Even those events I had written off as coincidence were an expression of divine love. Universal love. Love was an active, living force. It had always been there for me. All I needed to do was open my eyes and see and choose it.

It's not, I realized, that the lessons are about love. The lessons themselves *are* love. They are the journey to the heart.

I got up. And I let go of my balloon, watching it trail far up into the sky.

Understanding love didn't make the pain go away. Understanding love freed my heart.

It didn't mean I'd never feel pain again. An open heart feels pain and loss as well as love and joy. An open heart feels all it needs to feel. Otherwise, it closes again.

Thank you for my life, I whispered into the air.

I was surprised. At last I meant it.

# Thirteen

After all, magic is just a change in consciousness.

—JAMIE SAMS AND DAVID CARSON,
*MEDICINE CARDS*

I WALK INTO THE LIVING ROOM. NICHOLE IS sitting on the floor, rummaging through her box of photos. She's clipping pictures from magazines, then gluing them to a large piece of white cardboard.

She's making a project for psychology class: a poster to represent her life.

There are pictures of me, her brother, and the three of us. Pictures of Joey, Carmen, Ingrid, Ray. A photo of her dad. A parrot, gray with red tail feathers. And a skier soaring through the air.

In the middle of the poster she's pasted these words: LIFE'S BEEN GOOD TO ME SO FAR.

Nichole had been so worried about getting her grades up and whether she'd get accepted into college. She had thought she'd have to write a long letter telling what happened. Didn't know if that would work. But her grades had gone up, and she'd scored so high on her ACT tests that the college of her choice accepted her without any letter of explanation.

She taped the acceptance letter on the refrigerator.

The rest of the Get Along Gang still bursts into the house. Joey's making plans to go to college. Recently she came home from a conference, wrapped her arms around Nichole, hugged her, and said, "I don't care if your room is messy all the time. I love you." She found true love, all right. Found it all around her. The conference she attended was about opening your heart. Ingrid still has sparks in her eyes. She's planning for college, thinking about how much she'll miss her mom. Carmen says she's not sure if she'll go to college this year or the next. But she'll figure it out. And she's still baking caramel rolls.

I smile at their energy, their zest for life, and twist the ring on my finger. Yes, the golden poesy ring from Scotty. I'm becoming more comfortable opening my heart. I probably will lose everyone at some time. Or they'll lose me. Or the relationship will change or alter its course. But that's not a good enough reason to live in fear and push people away. Maybe my fear is telling me something: that I've opened my heart and let people in, I'm loving again.

I miss Shane. I always will. But something

new has happened. I'm learning to accept missing him.

We really do have it all. Every moment of every day. Now I know purpose comes from living out all those moments, enjoying them to the fullest.

I've traveled far and wide in the world, looking for holy places, spiritual places. I enjoy visiting them, but I've learned it's not necessary to look that hard or that far. The spiritual places are right here around me all the time—favorite restaurants, the kitchen, my room, Nichole's room, even my office. Those are the places of the heart.

I faced death. Didn't want to, but I did. Now I'm facing life. I know this. I'm committed to being here. And as long as I'm here I want to be full of passion for life.

And I know I don't have to look nearly as hard for my soul mates as I thought I did. They're the people in my life, the ones who help me learn my lessons, the lessons of love.

. . . . . . .

The last lesson in this story came from Ray, the only male member of the Get Along Gang. He was the one with two dreams. He wanted to be the best player ever on the Stillwater High School football team. And he wanted to find a way to go to college.

I walked into the living room one night about ten o'clock. Nichole was sitting in front of the television.

"Come here quick," she said.

I watched the screen. A sports announcer from Minneapolis stood on the Stillwater football field, interviewing Ray. They showed clips of him running the length of the field for a touchdown. They had named him player of the week.

"Haven't you heard?" Nichole said. "Ray is magic this year. He's a star!"

She told me he was doing so well that college football recruiters were here scouting him, urging him to apply to their schools.

I picked up the phone and called him. "This is great," I said. "I'm so happy for you, I want to buy you flowers. Take you to dinner. Do something."

"Why don't you?" he said.

So I did. I took him to dinner. And on homecoming night I brought three dozen yellow roses, one for each member of the football team. I gave Ray a card and told him how much I loved him, how happy I was for him. "You're magic, honey," I said. "Enjoy every moment, because you deserve it. And if the magic should ever leave, remember this: you know how to make your own."

I went to the football game that night, deliberately standing apart from Nichole and her friends. This was their event. I leaned on the fence and watched. I had been too miserable to attend social events when I was a child, so this was my first homecoming game. I giggled, listening to the buzz of the crowd. Waves of excitement rippled through the air as the cheerleaders jumped up and down and the "Star Spangled Banner" played over the loudspeaker. I sipped my hot chocolate. The game had begun.

The players lined up in the center of the field. The kickoff. We caught the ball at our six-yard line. Almost the whole length of the field to go for a touchdown. I took another sip of chocolate.

The ball was snapped.

"Number 1, Ray Wilhelm, has the ball!"

I watched as the figure darted past and

through the players. Someone tried to tackle him. He spun, broke free, kept running.

"He's at the twenty! The thirty! The fifty!"

The slender, lithe figure broke away from the cluster of players around him. He pulled ahead into the distance, running alone. When he crossed the goal line, the crowd jumped to its feet.

"Running ninety-four yards for a touchdown! Ray Wilhelm! For the Stillwater Ponies!"

The crowd roared. I screamed. Clapped so hard my hands stung.

And then amidst the cheering, screaming, whistling crowd, I heard it, heard it as clear as can be.

**This one's for you, Mom.**

I looked around. The night was lit by the stadium lights. A soft snow drifted down. The moon was out, a big chunk of white moon.

And in that moment, it looked to me like the universe was a beautiful big snow globe, one that encircled us all.

I would like to thank the following people for their cooperation in the creation of this book:

Louis Anderson
Nichole Beattie
Echo Bodine
Michael Bodine
Robert and Mary Cook
John Hanson and his parents,
Sue and Jim Hanson
Ingrid Haslund and her mother,
Dana Haslund
Ahmos Hassan
Izetta Lee
Scott Mengshol
Joey Nelson and her parents,
Susan and Roger Nelson
Carmen Pouncy and her father,
Willie Pouncy
Bob Severns and the Healing Heart Center
Anastasia Lynn Shinners-Peasley
Ray Wilhelm

# About the Author

Melody Beattie is the best-selling author of *Codependent No More*, *The Language of Letting Go*, and several other books. She lives with her daughter in a small town on the banks of Minnesota's St. Croix River.

Walker and Company Large Print books
are available from your local bookstore.
Please ask for them.
If you want to be on our mailing list to receive
a catalog and information about our titles,
please send your name and address to:

Beth Walker
Walker and Company
435 Hudson Street
New York, New York  10014

## Among the titles available are:

**GOOD MORNING, HOLY SPIRIT**
Benny Hinn

**CATHOLIC PRAYER BOOK**

**A GATHERING OF HOPE**
Helen Hayes

**WORDS TO LOVE BY**
Mother Teresa

**THE PROPHET**
Kahlil Gibran

**GIFT FROM THE SEA**
Anne Morrow Lindbergh

**THE GREATEST STORY EVER TOLD**
Fulton Oursler

**APPLES OF GOLD**
Jo Petty

**THE POWER OF POSITIVE THINKING**
Norman Vincent Peale

**THE ROAD LESS TRAVELED**
M. Scott Peck

**PRACTICE OF THE PRESENCE OF GOD**
Brother Lawrence

**MOTHER ANGELICA'S ANSWERS NOT PROMISES**
Mother Angelica

**LOVE IS A GENTLE STRANGER**
June Masters Bacher

**TO HELP YOU THROUGH THE HURTING**
Marjorie Holmes

**GUIDEPOSTS TREASURY OF CHRISTMAS**

**A BOOK OF ANGELS**
Sophy Burnham

**LOVE'S SILENT SONG**
June Masters Bacher

**PEACE, LOVE & HEALING**
Bernie S. Siegel

**THREE STEPS FORWARD, TWO STEPS BACK**
Charles R. Swindoll

**JESUS, THE WORD TO BE SPOKEN**
Mother Teresa

**SOMETHING BEAUTIFUL FOR GOD**
Malcolm Muggeridge

**PRAYERS AND PROMISES FOR EVERY DAY**
Corrie ten Boom

**GETTING THROUGH THE NIGHT**
Eugenia Price

**THE GRACE AWAKENING**
Charles Swindoll

**A GRIEF OBSERVED**
C. S. Lewis

**HOPE FOR THE TROUBLED HEART**
Billy Graham

**LAUGH AGAIN**
Charles Swindoll

**MAKING ALL THINGS NEW**
Henri J. M. Nouwen

**IRREGULAR PEOPLE**
Joyce Landorf

**AND THE ANGELS WERE SILENT**
Max Lucado

**RUTH**
Lois T. Henderson

**NOT I, BUT CHRIST**
Corrie ten Boom

**WORDS OF CERTITUDE**
Pope John Paul II

**LYDIA**
Lois Henderson

**THE WILL OF GOD**
Leslie Weatherhead

**BOOK OF HOURS**
Elizabeth Yates

**JEWISH WISDOM**
David and Esther Gross

**INTRODUCING THE BIBLE**
William Barclay

**GENESEE DIARY**
Henri J. M. Nouwen

**BE NOT AFRAID**
Alanson Houghton

**HOPE AND FAITH FOR TOUGH TIMES**
Robert H. Schuller

**WHERE IS GOD WHEN IT HURTS**
Philip Yancey

**THE GREATEST SALESMAN IN THE WORLD**
Og Mandino

**GOLDEN TREASURY OF PSALMS AND
PRAYERS**
Edna Beilenson

**REACHING OUT**
Henri J. M. Nouwen

**WHO NEEDS GOD**
Harold Kushner

**TWO-PART INVENTION**
Madeleine L'Engle

**ENCOURAGE ME**
Charles Swindoll